Bright Conquest

R·L·H

Ruth Livingston Hill
Bright Conquest

HARVEST HOUSE PUBLISHERS
Eugene, Oregon 97402

BRIGHT CONQUEST

Copyright © 1951 by Ruth H. Munce
Published by Harvest House Publishers
Eugene, Oregon 97402

ISBN 0-89081-524-0

Printed in the United States of America.

Bright
Conquest

CHAPTER I

THE MORNING WAS bleak and windy. Mrs. Williams pulled her worn fur coat about her closer as she crossed the bare brown fields near her snug home. Slowly as if with distaste, she approached a lonely frame dwelling in sparse woods by the side of a reedy lake. She unlocked the door of the ugly house and entered. Surveying the dreary disheveled room she gave a little shiver and shook her head with a pitying sigh.

"Such a place!" She spoke vehemently to the echoes of the empty house. "And it wasn't as if Morton Blackstone hadn't provided enough so his wife could make it a bright spot for him and the poor wee boy! It's just shiftless and philanderin' she was, that Myrtle Blackstone. I spose I'm sinful to think it, but I'm downright glad she's dead!" She nodded her head and two daring pink spots came out on her soft cheeks. *"If* she is!" she added with a shudder.

Mrs. Williams was a small gray-haired gentle-looking woman. Her hands moved capably and swiftly as she drew out one sagging drawer after another of the unpainted dresser in a small bedroom and emptied the meagre contents into a suitcase she had brought. Boy's things, they were, and all needing repairs of some sort.

Her work was soon finished and she went quickly out, locking the door behind her as if she were glad to be in the fresh air once more.

"It'll be many a day, perhaps," she thought to herself, "before this door is opened again. Poor man! I guess it's good that his life has been spared, but twenty years is still a long time." She sighed with compassion as she took the footpath across the wintry brown field between the ugly narrow house she had left and her own cosy brown cottage. A brave crocus peeped at her from the yard and she smiled, her mind busy with loving plans.

"I'll have these bit things all mended and ready when Roger boy arrives. And, let's see, I guess chicken with dumplings would be a nice supper for him the first night here!" She nodded to herself in happy anticipation. It would be good to have a boy to mother again. It would help to ease the old pang of emptiness that had been in her heart ever since the navy department had sent that message about her own boy during the war. There would be some of his playthings that this poor child would enjoy. His skates, and his baseball things. Oh, it would be good to watch the joy come back into little Roger Blackstone's eyes. There would be heartaches, yes, but a body had to have those in some form anyway, so why not have a good reason for them in the shape of a poor motherless little boy whose father was to spend twenty years behind bars! The tears came to her eyes again as she thought how she would try to cheer the little nine-year-old and feed him and love him.

But as Mrs. Williams opened her own door, closing it quickly after her against the March wind, she was aware that there was another person in the house. She braced herself.

There sitting in her own rocker before the fire was her niece-by-marriage, Alberta Sneller, knitting composedly on a cerise bouclé suit.

Alberta's prominent beady eyes pierced her aunt accusingly directing a glare at the suitcase she carried.

Mrs. Williams girt up her loins and summoned a smile, but it was not the same smile that had rested lightly on her lips before she came into the house.

"Why, good morning, Alberta," she said pleasantly, "I'm surprised to see you so early. I supposed you would be busy all day getting ready for your club tea this afternoon. How is everything going? Were the cookies I sent over all right? I'm glad you asked me to help. You know I'm not much on clubs, but I realize that you have your hands full and it's nice for an old woman like me to feel that I can take a little burden off other people's shoulders now and then!"

Mrs. Williams talked brightly, hoping to stall off the storm she surmised was brewing in Alberta's large and tightly girt bosom. She was not certain yet just what form the storm would take but she could guess, especially if Alberta suspected the reason for her early visit to the house across the fields.

Mrs. Williams set the suitcase down unostentatiously behind the door of a small room adjoining the living room and made no reference to it although Alberta's look betrayed her thirst for an explanation.

"I *am* busy, of course, Aunt Ag," snapped Alberta. "But there are *some* things that take precedence over teas. One of them is the matter of family *honor* and *reputation*. I may as well come to the point. You know I never *was* one for beating around the bush!"

Mrs. Williams raised her graying eyebrows a little. She wished that her niece's last sentence were not so true.

"The rumor has come to me, never mind how," blurted out Alberta, her angry fingers clicking faster than ever, "that you have taken leave of your *senses* to the extent that you are actually planning to take that un*speak*able Blackstone boy into your home and *slave* for him!" Every bobby pin in Alberta Sneller's carefully set hair seemed to be aimed in venom straight at Mrs. Williams' gentle gray eyes.

Agnes Williams' face lit up with a veritable light of pleasure although a light of battle might have been discerned there as well. She said nothing, only waited.

That exasperated Alberta whose strong point in battle was

parrying the enemy's thrusts before they were scarce begun. An enemy who stood still, apparently unharmed by the first blow, was annoying.

"Aside from the fact that you are *old*," Alberta made no attempt to soften the word, "and that you have just lost your husband and will have all the burden of supporting yourself, you think that you can take on a child, a mere *infant,* who is as good as orphaned. I've never heard any good of that boy. He's always into mischief. With such parents as his, he'll *never* be *anything* but a headache to you. More than that, it is a positive disgrace to the family! After the *countrywide* publicity that has been given to the whole terrible case, to have our names connected with it all over again is nothing short of insult."

"Oh, do you think so?" responded Mrs. Williams innocently. "I hadn't thought of it that way."

"No. Of course you wouldn't. You never *do* think of what folks say. How do you think I can hold up my head before my friends this afternoon with all of them knowing that you as much as *sympathize* with *murder!*"

"Well, Alberta," replied Mrs. Williams, stiffening a little, "I suppose you know how I feel. I have never been convinced that it was murder."

"It's a pity you hadn't been on the jury, then!" she spat out sarcastically. "They all seemed to differ with you. And you don't seem to realize that you are slandering my husband who proved the case when you talk like that. I hope to goodness you aren't going to go around and give out that kind of sentimental *nonsense!*"

Alberta was fairly screaming and Mrs. Williams wore a troubled look.

"I still can't reconcile such a thing with what we all know of Morton Blackstone, Alberta," she said. "He has always been a sober, industrious, upright man. He had a lot to put up with from his wife but he did put up with it, for years. It doesn't stand to reason that all at once he would shove her in the lake. As far as any evidence shows, she hadn't been carryin' on especially at the time. No, it just doesn't make sense."

Mrs. Williams was talking quietly, as if reasoning the whole case out to herself regardless of her visitor. But Alberta blazed at her.

"Absurd! Don't you know that Dick could have you brought up for *libel* or—or something, if you try to tear down his professional *integrity* like that? He *proved* that Morton Blackstone drowned his wife."

Mrs. Williams looked tired. "I'm sorry to hurt you, Alberta," she apologized patiently. "I forgot for the moment that Dick had anything to do with it. I just—"

"You *forgot!*" burst in Alberta. "That's *impossible*. When Dick was the prosecuting attorney, the most important figure in the *whole trial!* Positively, Aunt Ag, sometimes I think you are getting childish. It's your age, I suppose, and I must learn to be patient. But I declare, some things are pretty hard to take! I suppose you just can't keep up with what's going on any more. But that's another reason why I must in*sist* that you do not take this awful boy. Dick says so too. He says you can't tell what legal involvements you may bring on yourself, that *he* will have to try to straighten out for you. In fact, Dick asked me to come over here and talk to you."

Mrs. Williams looked steadily at her niece a moment and then turned her eyes to the deserted bleak house across the fields. When she brought her glance back it rested on a framed motto over her fireplace: "Thou wilt keep him in perfect peace whose mind is stayed on Thee."

She drew a deep breath and smiled again.

"Well, I'm sorry if you and Dick disapprove," she said quietly. "I've signed the guardianship papers, though, and I shall not go back on my word."

Alberta bristled.

"But didn't you *know* that you could have got the boy into an orphanage? I'm sure Dick gives enough to our denominational institutions so that he ought to get some good out of them. He sends them twenty-five dollars *twice* a year. He has to, you know, since he is on the board of directors. It wouldn't look well if he didn't."

Mrs. Williams veiled her eyes and looked away again. She did not care to mention that of her much smaller income she gave six times that amount to the orphanage. She shut her lips tight, then after a moment she looked squarely at her niece and asked,

"Would you like to grow up in an orphanage, Alberta?"

Alberta flushed. "Certainly not," she snapped, "and neither would you. But I think it's a good thing there *are* such places for children who are so unfortunate as not to have *law-abiding* parents."

Mrs. Williams' eye took on a wicked twinkle.

"How many nights do you suppose the boy sat up deciding he'd not be born to good parents?" she asked mischievously.

"Aunt *Agnes!*" reproved Alberta belligerently. "It seems to me that you are taking this *whole* matter too lightly. I certainly did not expect to be made *fun* of when I came over here in all kindness to try to help you to see things from the right angle."

Mrs. Williams laughed.

"I meant no harm, child," she soothed. "Only let's not have such a to-do over it. The whole thing will blow over soon."

"You are mistaken. It will not. The town is roused. *Everyone* is talking. You simply don't *know* what you are getting into."

Alberta blustered and raged, reminding her aunt that Mona, the daughter for whom she was knitting, would enter high school shortly and implying that Mona's social assets would be endangered when the news got around that Mona's aunt practically sympathized with murder! But Mrs. Williams held her ground.

As a last plea, Alberta offered the threat that the worthless boy in question would be sure to grow up and make off with all of

Mrs. Williams' worldly goods and that would be the final blow
to the hopes of her own niece's family.

But Mrs. Williams remained calm. With a shrug she responded,

"I haven't so very much to lose, anyway, you know, Alberta.
By the way," she welcomed an opportunity to change the subject, "I had a letter from Polly today and she told me some of
the cutest things that little Wynelle said. I must get it and read
them to you."

She rose to hasten into her bedroom for the letter but Alberta
was on her feet and stopped her.

"No, I haven't time to hear any letters today. I see I have failed
to make you understand *what* you are doing to us all. You will
find out to your sorrow some day. There may be repercussions
that can affect even your precious granddaughter Wynelle. I'm
sure I *hope* it won't be as bad as we fear but I don't see how you
think you can do it. Good-by now." She thrust her knitting into
an ugly brown bag with bright green plastic handles and went
out without further ceremony.

Mrs. Williams stared after her a few moments with a troubled
look then shook her head after the indignant retreating back
of her niece.

"Well," she mused, "it's possible that it may be as difficult as
you fear. Yes, it's quite possible. But," she added as she turned
back to her housework with determination, "I expect to do it until
I die, or for the next ten or fifteen years, anyway."

CHAPTER 2

It was more than ten and almost fifteen years later that Wynelle Williams closed and locked the dingy door of the coal company office where she had stayed late to wait for the last driver to return. With a sigh she started down the grimy uneven brick walk that would lead her the six hot blocks to the ugly brick house where she shared a room with her mother in her married sister's home.

She planted her pretty feet one before the other almost resentfully. The sun glared too brightly to look up and so she looked down at the walk thinking, "I hate you, I hate you! How much longer am I going to have to take this horrid path? I've *always* hated you! Will I never get free of you? This ugly little town! There's nobody here who is the slightest bit interesting to me. It's not that I'm anything out of the ordinary, but I would like it if just one interesting person would turn up, some time. There isn't a soul who cares about anything worth while. The women plan what they will have for dinner, and whether their new curtains will be green or blue; the girls discuss their dates with the drips that are as dull as they are. And the boys! Oh, why couldn't there be just one interesting boy or man in this whole dinky little place!"

Her mind darted from one to another of the men who had aspired to a more than passing acquaintance with her.

There was Bud Hendricks. He worked in a garage and his too-long drab hair was always greasy looking. Wynelle did not consider herself above a hard-working mechanic. His hard work was the best thing about him. But it had soon become evident,

14

after the first half hour of her first date with him, that his greatest ambition was to acquire for his miserable old jalopy every possible accessory that could be affixed thereto. When Wynelle would try to bring up any subject outside their own town doings, he seemed deaf and merely proposed another soda, selecting a comic book to read while they waited for it. Wynelle had endured two evenings with him and then she had been too busy helping her sister with the baby to go again.

Black-haired Harry Harper, gay and smiling, had asked her for a date once. She always suspected that he must have made a bet that he would date every girl in town at least once, otherwise he never would have picked on her, for their tastes did not converge at any point. He wanted to take her to a show that was already raising indignation among the decent people of the town. And when they finally compromised on an evening of roller skating she found that he held her too closely and kept telling her stories that were not nice. On the way home he stopped at a tap room as a matter of course and when she refused to go in he grew angry and practically insulted her before they reached her home. He never asked her again for which she was thankful.

Lambert Odum, the clerk in the coal office, was not like that. But of the two Wynelle almost preferred Harry. Lammie, as he was generally termed, was what Wynelle called soupy. He had large pale eyes and long pale hands that were always damp. His chin looked as if it had been tucked away under his collar. He composed poetry and continually quoted it to her with meaningful glances that disgusted and embarrassed her. He would leave poems on her typewriter at the office and the boss would find them and tease her. Oh, how she loathed Lambert!

There were others whom she had tried to like; for the most part they were boys she had been to school with, but she had always loved books and none of them did. They were overawed by her bright mind. Every time she attempted to exercise her keen wits or lighten the boredom of their company with humor, it left them floundering and herself embarrassed and discouraged.

It seemed as if no intelligent, well-set-up young man—she had dropped the requisite of good looks as least important—would ever so much as show his face in the little town.

Wynelle was not boy crazy but she was nineteen and not unattractive. She was small, with soft wavy brown hair, brown eyes and clear skin. She was dainty and she had a nice smile. Yet she had never had what she would call an interesting or stimulating conversation with any personable young man. There was nobody who could help the situation either. At home, if she dropped her guard and allowed her thoughts to be evident, her mother would look troubled and her sister would look significantly at her husband and in a few days a dinner guest would be produced from among her brother-in-law's business associates, with an evening planned that would throw her in his company. Everyone would watch hopefully to see whether the two would take to each other. But as most of the men were older than Wynelle, and generally quite worldly, which Wynelle was not, she always sent them on their way without encouragement. Then there would be a family session behind closed doors and each of the adults would make remarks aimed at Wynelle for some days afterward, either extolling the virtues of the recent guest or implying that Wynelle was not in a position to be so everlastingly particular about her boy friends. After that Wynelle would decide to keep her mouth shut and hide her thoughts within herself.

Occasionally during the last lonely year she had toyed with the idea of going east to visit her grandmother Williams. But the way had never seemed to open and now her grandmother was dead. Wynelle was sorry. She had always felt a longing to know her when her brief sweet letters would come at infrequent intervals. She had always seemed to Wynelle so much more like a real mother than her own mother was. It was no wonder that her grandmother's kind heart had moved her to take in a poor motherless boy some years ago. That was considered by the whole family as a sign of Mrs. Williams' erraticism, but Wynelle had always thought it a lovely thing to do, though of course she had never seen the boy. Her grandmother must have been aware of the family disapproval, for she rarely mentioned him in her letters. Now and then she would say "Roger graduated from high school with honors this week," or "Roger has enlisted in the Air Corps, he is young but I'm glad he wants to serve." That was late in the second world war. The last thing Grandmother Williams had written was that Roger was finishing his law course. But Wynelle's mother never paid much attention to her mother-in-law's news, and always gave a little contemptuous frown when the boy was mentioned.

"It does seem as if mother might have made a little more fuss over her own grandchildren," she said once, "and not poured out all her affection and her money on a worthless stranger-child."

A remark like that hurt Wynelle, even when she was very young, for her heart was tender toward lonely unwanted children. She had never been really happy herself since her father had died. She and her mother had little in common, although her mother required her constant presence with her.

As she reached home she felt as if she were about at the end of her rope. Lately she had weighed the wisdom of taking the three hundred dollars she had saved up working for the coal company to sally forth perhaps to New York City itself, and seek her fortune. Many girls were doing it nowadays. But she had sense enough to know that three hundred dollars would not carry her far and if she had difficulty getting work she would have been far better off back in Uniontown at her sister's, unpleasant as conditions were, than starving in a big city with no friends near. So she would take a deep sighing breath and decide to stick it out a little longer until she could save more or until something else turned up. But the loneliness grew.

There was little relief from the blistering heat when she stepped inside her sister's squeaking screen door. The house was not insulated and each brick seemed fairly smoldering. The baby was crying an insistent petulant wail. A strong unpleasant odor hung in the air. Sauer kraut again!

She mopped her wet forehead, glancing on her way up the narrow stairs at the spot beside the cheap gilt clock where letters were always placed. She was anxious to get up and get her things off and splash in some cool water a few minutes, that is, if Arthur, her brother-in-law, were not there ahead of her. He always took a long and luxurious bath especially if he happened to be going out in the evening.

She had climbed four steps before her tired eyes managed to convey to her mind that there actually was a letter there beside the clock on the mantelpiece. It might be for her. Everyone else was at home and would surely have claimed their letters by now. With a faint flutter of hope that some circumstance, however small, might wedge its way into the dark fortress of her dreary life, Wynelle skipped down the four steps again and reached for the letter.

It was for her, and bore in the upper left corner the name of a law firm in the town where her grandmother had lived until her recent death.

Wondering why the lawyers should be writing to her instead of to her mother, Wynelle paused on the stair-landing to read her letter. None of the family were in evidence at the moment, and she would much prefer to receive any news all by herself if possible. Even her mother would ask prying loving questions while she read. She would like to be in command of the situation before she was required to answer any questions at all. Of course it would be nothing of any interest. Perhaps an advertisement. But why on earth would lawyers on the east coast want to advertise to her their skill in solving problems? Oh, very likely it was some circular or legal announcement that each one of her grandmother's family had received. That must be it. Still, it was nice to be getting some kind of letter for herself.

She tore it open. It was a personal letter.

It is our pleasant duty to inform you that you have been named in the will of your grandmother Mrs. Agnes Williams as the heir to her property located at 119 Summit Street, Maple Grove, Virginia.

The place is old and may need quite a bit of repair. It can hardly hope to bring much either at a sale or as income property. As you would no doubt find it difficult to arrange a trip east, we would be glad to take over for you the business details of the matter. In our opinion, it would be wise to dispose of the property at the best price and if you agree to our handling it, will you kindly sign the enclosed form and return it at your earliest convenience. You may safely trust the discretion of our staff to guard your interests in the matter.

Very truly yours,

Richard E. Sneller, Atty.

P.S. Give our regards to all the family. Dick S.

The last sentence was scribbled by hand.

As Wynelle read the words, hastily the first time, then carefully over and over again, a slow pink stole up in her cheeks and her breath came faster. Her eyes widened and sought the cramped horizon beyond the next brick house. Then all at once the brick houses and the sauer kraut and the baby's wails were no more. She was standing in a shabby living room two thousand miles away, surveying her own domain! Its walls were fairly crumbling, so that in her fancy there were actually places where the daylight shone through, but it was hers, and perhaps it could be mended. It was home!

Within her heart Wynelle knew that somehow she was going to make that trip which her cousin Dick seemed to think unnecessary. It might be wiser, perhaps, to let lawyers handle the affair, especially as one of them was her own second cousin's husband, but lawyers did not know how she felt. This was the chance she had been looking and longing for so long. Maple Grove might turn out to be just as dinky and uninteresting a town as Uniontown, her present home, but at least it would be different, and there would be something there that was hers, with which she could do as she pleased. For the first time since she was a child Wynelle felt free and lighthearted.

She fairly skipped up the stairs to her room, where she found her mother lying down with one of her headaches. Suppressing her own excitement, Wynelle went about ministering to her mother, almost ashamed of the feeling of joy in her own heart when her mother was so miserable. She decided not to say anything about the letter until her mother was better.

But at supper her sister brought up the subject and asked her point blank what her letter was about and why she was hearing from Carey and Sneller. Wynelle tried her best to look casual. She was glad her mother was not down to supper, for she would have pried every word of the letter from her. Her sister would ask and then let it drop, probably, simply because she was more interested in her own affairs than in Wynelle's.

"Oh," Wynelle answered in an even tone, "our legal cousin wrote to let me know that Grandmother Williams has left me a little something in her will. I don't know just what it will amount to. Apparently not much."

"Well!" exclaimed her sister, not unpleasantly. "That's nice. I suppose that's because you are named Agnes Wynelle instead of Sarah Jane like me!" She laughed in a tired way. "Well, I'm glad to know grandmother didn't lose her interest in her own family completely just because she took that strange boy to raise. She always seemed so sold on him in her letters that I supposed everything would go to him. So we have an heiress in the family!" She said it banteringly.

"Nothing like that, I'm afraid," Wynelle laughed.

"Well, I hope you will get enough to buy yourself a bed, any-how," her sister responded bluntly. "When the baby arrives he'll have to use Johnny's crib. That means we would have to get a bed for Johnny and I don't see how we could manage it. "Honey," she went on turning to her husband who sat munching uninter-estedly at the other end of the table, "if Wyn can get a bed in time could you put a fresh coat of enamel on Johnny's crib? That will all work out very nicely."

Arthur grunted assent and hurried on with his dinner. He had to go out to bowl that evening with his office team.

Wynelle was glad that her sister had to see to Johnny right after supper, leaving her to do the dishes alone. She did not care to talk this thing over just yet. She slipped quietly into bed later that evening without disturbing her mother who had fallen into a restless moaning sleep. The letter she tucked under her pillow along with the little soft leather book of daily Bible readings that her grandmother had sent her the year before. Wynelle prized the book. She had comparatively little knowledge of the Bible, though she had always attended church and Sunday School. But she had a sort of trust in God's caring for her and these daily verses had encouraged her. They seemed to be arranged for her special need, time after time. Now she had a feeling that the letter belonged with the book because it seemed like a confirma-tion of some of the promises.

She fell to wondering again what the house would be like. Her grandmother never had been one to send snapshots or give much description of her life and activities. A mere word that she was well or a little gift occasionally was about all they heard from her. So Wynelle did not have even a picture of the house to build up dreams upon.

She determined that the very next day she would inquire about the price of tickets and even if she had to take the long trip by bus, if that were much cheaper, she would leave for Maple Grove as soon as she could possibly get ready. Her mother might demur but Wynelle felt that this was something that she really had a right to take into her own hands. Besides would it not be a real easing of the situation in her sister's home if she were out of the way? There would be no need then to spend money on getting a new bed. For Wynelle had far back in her own mind a little reserve decision that if the new town promised any work and any interest at all above what she had known in Uniontown, she would stay. She was a good stenographer and could keep excellent books. There was no reason why she should not be able to get a good job. And with a home already prepared for her what more could she ask? Of course it might not do to live there all alone, but she could surely rent a room to some nice elderly lady, or another business girl like herself. Or maybe one of her own cousins would like to come and live with her. She was not sure of their ages. She recalled that there was a daughter Mona, older than herself, who had already been married and divorced; a son about her own age and two younger daughters. She knew very little about them.

Maple Grove was a pasture beyond her own fence, and it looked far greener than her old Uniontown pasture, at least from this distance.

The next morning Wynelle was up long before her mother awoke. She had been quietly going over her small stock of clothing, sorting the things she would need on her trip, laying the rest in her bottom drawer to be packed and sent to her later if she decided to stay in Maple Grove. She would say nothing here about that secret purpose of hers. It would be sure to be contested, for no reason except that it was something out of the ordinary. Wynelle was under no delusions about her family's love for her. Oh, they cared for her in a casual way but they had always told Wynelle that she was like her father, and her mother seemed to resent that. Sarah Jane was fond of her sister and would never let her actually suffer for food or shelter, of course, but she was wrapped up in her own family and Wynelle could not help guessing that it was quite a trial for her and Arthur to have relatives sharing their tiny home. It was wonderful to be given this chance to get away and start afresh legitimately, without having to leave stealthily and then perhaps fail to make good and have to come creeping home again.

Suddenly Mrs. Williams awoke and demanded in a sort of loving whine, "What on earth are you doing, Wynelle?"

"Oh, are you awake, mother? How do you feel this morning? Is your head any better?"

"Well, maybe a little." The tired voice sounded so discouraged that Wynelle had a guilty feeling that it was wrong of her to be planning to go off from all her family and leave her mother to suffering. But her mother would be better off. She would have the whole room to herself and anyway Sarah Jane and she were really congenial. They loved to discuss which pattern they would use for Johnny's new rompers, and whether he would look nice in yellow with his reddish curls. Wynelle was fond of her little nephew, but it seemed as if there were no place for her to fit in. She hugged her plan to herself and snuggled her letter into her handbag until she finished dressing.

She hesitated about telling her news. Her mother would have so much to say about it. Wynelle dreaded a lot of talk. Why couldn't she just up and leave some morning, without any ado about it? But families did like to discuss affairs and she knew they would all feel resentful if they did not know all the details of her going so that they could recount them with relish at the next gathering they attended. She might as well get it over with as soon as possible. If she didn't tell her mother and Sarah Jane did, there would be a big time over it. Her mother would ask why it was she had kept it from her. So she went over to her mother's bed and sat down on the edge with a smile.

"Did you know I got a letter from Cousin Dick Sneller,

mother?" she began, with the same feeling she always had when she stepped into a cold bath.

Her mother's pale blue eyes opened swiftly and looked at her keenly.

"No, I didn't," answered Mrs. Williams querulously. "What on earth did he want of you? They aren't coming to visit, are they?" she cried in alarm.

"No, nothing like that," laughed Wynelle. "He wrote from his office telling me that Grandmother Williams had left me her house." A note of exultation crept into her voice in spite of her.

Mrs. Williams pushed back her straggling gray hair, tossed from her day and night of misery, and raised herself up on one elbow.

"You don't mean it!" she cried. "Well, I'm glad to hear it. I thought she'd forgotten us all. How much is the house worth, did Dick say?"

"No, but he said it wouldn't be much. It needs repairs."

"I can imagine. You'd think that boy she took to raise would have the gratitude to help keep it up, but very likely she spoiled him. It was a crazy idea for her to take him at her age, especially with no man to help her. I suppose she spent what little she ever had on him, and there's nothing but the house left. I'm glad she had the grace to remember you. She seemed so pleased when I wrote that we had named you after her. I wonder how much she had when she died. She never said much in her letters. I declare, sometimes it has been hard to understand her, although I did feel bad that I couldn't get there when she died. But it was so sudden and it would have cost so much. We couldn't have made it in time for the funeral either."

Wynelle disliked to hear her mother continually make excuses for her long neglect of Grandmother Williams. Wynelle had wanted to go east to the funeral herself, but her mother would not hear of it. There was no need, she said. Her grandmother was not there any more and Alberta could manage everything just as well. Alberta had always been so nice to Grandmother Williams. It was a comfort to feel that she was there, one of the family.

Wynelle wondered at herself taking matters in her own hands and planning to go now without consulting anybody. The acquisition of property of her own had suddenly made her feel independent. Probably she would find that her inheritance was little more than a shack when she got there, but at least she would have the trip and she felt as if she just must get away, soon.

"I'm going east to see the house, mother," announced Wynelle quietly, giving her hair a last brush.

"Going east!" exclaimed her mother sitting up in bed. "Are you crazy? Don't you know you'll spend more than you'll get for the little old house? I doubt if it amounts to anything at all. She probably had a big mortgage on it, and if it needs repair you'll have nothing but bills for your trouble. No, my dear, you must not think of it. That would not be wise at all. You just let Cousin Dick Sneller handle the whole thing. Don't let a little thing like your name in somebody's will make you lose your good sense. You haven't inherited a fortune, I'm quite sure of that!"

But Wynelle only smiled. There was no further need to argue. She had made her announcement. There would be sure to be discussion by the rest over what she ought to do. Still, she could go right on and plan and carry out her plans. Nobody could say she had acted in an underhanded manner.

Her mother talked on, reminiscing mostly, about the one time she had been in her mother-in-law's little brown house, years ago, before Sarah Jane was born.

"It seemed terribly old-fashioned, even then, I remember. I don't recall what it was built of but it gave me the impression of being just a little brown shack shut off among the trees. I never did like that feeling. I like to live close to neighbors, nice ones, of course, but to have them near enough to call to at night, or chat with over the back fence mornings. I wanted the folks to take a little new brick house nearer to the shipping district but somehow they had set their hearts on this old thing out near the edge of town. I shouldn't wonder if the whole neighborhood there was worthless now. It wasn't built up much even then. The only house I recall was a little ugly narrow clapboard thing across a field. I think that was where the man lived who later killed his wife, the one whose boy your grandmother took. Oh, I wonder why she never seemed to have good judgment. If she had only come to live with us out west here after the menfolks died she would have had Arthur to advise her. Of course, Dick Sneller was there in Maple Grove, but somehow she never did warm up to Dick and Alberta. Well, it's strange to have all this coming up now. It'll be interesting to see what comes of it. Nothing much, I suppose. Why are you hurrying off so early, Wynnie? I hoped you could have time to wash my hair and put it up in pin curls before you left for work this morning. Those ladies in Sarah Jane's sewing club are coming this afternoon and I look a fright."

Wynelle looked troubled, but she shook her head.

"I'm sorry, mother, I have a couple of errands to do," she said. "I didn't know you wanted your hair done, I thought you wouldn't be feeling up to it."

"Well, I'll have to be up and around this afternoon whether I feel like it or not, to help Sarah Jane. But never mind," she added a little coldly, "if you have other plans. I can struggle with it myself, I suppose, only it never does look as nice as when you do it."

"That's too bad, mother. I could have planned differently. But it's too late now to do it and get to the office on time."

"Oh, is it? Well, never mind," she said in an offended tone. "It doesn't matter about just me anyway. You go on and do your own errands."

"But mother, I couldn't do your hair, there isn't time now," reiterated Wynelle with a troubled pucker in her brow. "The errands won't take ten minutes. It takes at least forty-five to do your hair."

Her mother merely sank back on her pillow with a sigh and

waved her away. "Go on now and forget about me," she said coldly emphasizing the "me."

Wearily Wynelle went out and closed the door, stepping softly down the stairs so as not to waken the others. She poured herself a cup of coffee, left over from her sister and brother-in-law's early breakfast. Arthur left at seven and Sarah Jane always went back to bed for an hour or two if Johnny wasn't awake yet. A piece of hard cold toast half buttered, was on Wynelle's plate, and a tag end of cold greasy bacon lay abandoned among shreds of a scrambled egg. The food was placed before Wynelle's seat at the table; it was evident that she was meant to have it for her breakfast. She choked down a bite or two, washed her dishes and left the house as quickly as she could.

For the first time in years her feet flew eagerly down the dingy brick walks. She made various inquiries, took careful notes of what the different agents told her, and stowed them away in her bag to study in spare moments between her duties at the coal company.

She was not encouraged by her findings. The cost of the trip would be far more than she had anticipated. The only way she could hope to make it would be to go by bus and even that would require such a long time that meals would become an important item. She knew she could manage on very little, however, and she could take with her enough food for two or three meals. She was determined to go through with her plan. The return ticket worried her. If she took a round trip she could travel for less, but how did she know she was coming back? She was greatly tempted to take only a one-way ticket and trust that she could get a job during her stay that would help to buy her passage home if she decided to come back.

As for clothes, she determined that what she had already would have to do. She had a good lightweight navy suit with several blouses and they should carry her along pretty well, with her dark blue print for a change. It would have been nice to arrive in fresh new things but she couldn't have the trip and new clothes too. She would just have to trust to careful grooming to keep herself from looking tacky. She did need a new pair of shoes though. Shabby shoes gave oneself away and she would like to look nice if she met her eastern cousins or—well, some young man! She grimaced at herself. How ridiculous for her even to imagine such a thing. Young men were not waiting by the roadside for attractive girls with new shoes to come along. It was not likely that she would meet anybody more interesting than she had ever met right here in Uniontown. She despised girls who were out looking for a man. This was solely a business and refresher trip! Although, she admitted to herself, if a nice young man happened in her path she need not look the other way! But in that case, if he were *very* nice he wouldn't be caring whether her shoes were new or not.

During the day she found time to answer her cousin's letter telling him that she planned to come east and see her property, that she had been contemplating a trip for some time anyway, and would combine business and pleasure. She thanked him for offering to take charge of the matter for her, but she said that she would like to see the place before she decided whether to sell it or possibly fix it up and rent it to some good tenant.

When Wynelle reached home that night, she found the family in a furor of discussion about her.

"I think it would be a splendid thing for Wynnie to go, mother," insisted Sarah Jane.

Wynelle felt a little pang as she sensed that at least half the eagerness in her sister's voice was due to relief that her own little home would be less crowded. But Wynelle chose to disregard the hurt. Why shouldn't Sarah Jane be glad to be rid of her? The house certainly was crowded, and although Wynelle helped considerably with the housework and with Johnny, as well as paying her share of the expenses, she realized that if she had a husband and little boy of her own she would want to have it all to herself, too. So she smiled and welcomed her sister's support.

"But it's ridiculous, my dear," rejoined the mother, "to go traipsing off like that on account of a little shack that won't be worth the price of her ticket. People will think Wynnie has lost her head, or else get the idea that she has a great deal of money left her and that is never good. They expect so much of you then."

"Why worry over that? Wyn has a stupid time compared to lots of girls her age. I think she ought to go, whether there's any money involved or not."

Wynelle listened quietly as she patiently worked away at the chicken wing Arthur had served her, trying to get enough from it to last her until the next meal. She was about to open her mouth to state that she was definitely going east and there was no use in anyone trying to stop her, when all of a sudden Arthur spoke. He did not usually enter into conversation at the table. He let the womenfolk do the chatting while he ate glumly and excused himself early as often as he could. Wynelle looked up surprised, disliking as much as ever his round bare forehead and his round stubby double chin that was always bristly black at this time of day.

"It's a good idea for her to go," he blurted out, as if that settled it, as indeed his word usually did.

Wynelle recognized again the relief it would be to her sister and brother if she were gone. But she was not prepared for what he said next.

"If she wants a free trip," he went on, referring as usual to his sister-in-law in the third person, "I think I can get her one. A man I know is flying east in his own plane and taking an invalid friend of his mother's. The woman needs somebody along, another woman, she says, to look out for her on the trip. He said today when he stopped in our office that if he could get somebody who would suit this lady that he would take 'em for nothing. Be a good chance for a free ride."

Wynelle caught her breath and her eyes lit up. Of all the modes of travel that she could have chosen, flying was the one that appealed to her the most. She had yearned for a long time to have a plane trip, but she had thought it out of the question because of the expense.

Now she said nothing in answer to her brother-in-law's proposal because her mother and sister immediately seized on it and began tossing it back and forth between them as if the matter were solely their own to decide.

"What would Wynelle know about caring for an invalid?" cried her mother. "What if the woman had a heart attack right on the plane? What if she *died*? Wynelle might be held responsible!"

"Oh mother, don't be such a Calamity Jane," remonstrated her elder daughter. "A woman would have medicines with her and she certainly wouldn't expect a casual stranger to be as good as a doctor."

And so it went. But after Arthur had excused himself according to his custom and gone out on the porch for a smoke, Wynelle slipped out stealthily between her trips to the kitchen with the dishes and asked him the name and address of the woman who was going east.

"I'd like to do that," she said quietly.

"Hunh!" assented Arthur in as pleasant tone as he ever used. "Okay. I'll tell 'im you'll try it." He gave her the address: "Mrs. R. K. Ardsley, 109 East Main St."

In a fever lest someone else might snap up the opportunity, Wynelle hurried through the dishes and dressed carefully. She slipped out the back door calling out that she might stop in and see Irene Chambers for a few minutes, not to worry about where she was.

Irene was a girl who worked in an office near the coal company and Wynelle sometimes had lunch with her at the little pie shop nearby. She thought of Irene as an alibi on the spur of the moment because she lived not far from the lady whose address Arthur had given her.

The old brick walk seemed fairly to level itself out under her eager feet as she sped along in the gathering dusk.

The group of old elm trees on the corner of Dr. Rutherford's lawn reached down tender fingers of sympathy and understanding, it seemed to her, as she passed under them. Those trees were the one thing she had really loved about Uniontown. For years they had shaded a little section of her walk to and from school. And on moonlit evenings, she had sometimes walked beneath them crying out silently her loneliness. She had a feeling that they were eager that she have this chance that she so longed for.

It was nearly a mile to the elderly lady's house, but Wynelle was a good walker and she arrived before Mrs. Ardsley had retired.

The old lady seemed anything but a frail invalid. She was only lame. It was evident that she took to Wynelle from the start. After a pleasant visit and questions on both sides, the trip was arranged.

"I will telephone Ed the first thing in the morning," promised Mrs. Ardsley. "He was anxious to leave the end of this week, because he wanted to be back as soon as possible. Could you be ready by then?"

"Oh yes," agreed Wynelle breathlessly. She could scarcely believe that her plan was really taking shape. It sounded so like what might happen to some other girl but not to herself.

She was so excited on the way home that she almost forgot to stop at Irene's, but she did look in, just in case the family checked on where she had been.

But Johnny was sick and feverish when she reached home and their minds were not on her, for which she was grateful. She wanted to be alone and think out the details of what she was to do. She was glad she had sent that letter to Dick Sneller by air mail. It might be awkward to arrive before he had even heard from her.

But when the letter arrived at the Sneller home it produced a degree of consternation.

CHAPTER 3

"THE GIRL IS likely one of these Smart Aleck teen-agers who think they know it all!" blustered Dick Sneller. "Why couldn't she be content to let me manage the sale of the house and stay put out there where she belongs? I'll have the whole thing to straighten out anyway. All she will do is mess it up and make it a lot harder to accomplish anything. Women! Always poking into things that aren't their business."

"I should think it *was* her business, dad," spoke up Dick's own bold teen-ager from her place at the side of the dinner table. "It's her house, isn't it? I would want to see it if it were mine. Why do you think *you* can guess what she wants to do with it?"

"Hold your tongue, Della," snapped her mother, "and don't be impudent to your father. Of course he knows what is best to do. A lot more, indeed, than a silly young girl who has probably lost her head over the idea of inheriting something, even though it doesn't amount to much."

"Doesn't amount to much!" retorted Della disregarding her mother's command. "I thought I heard dad tell you he wouldn't mind having the house himself, that it was a snug, well-built old place, and would bring a good rent from people who are willing to pay a lot for something artistic. I'm sure I heard you say that, dad."

"What if I did!" snarled Dick. "Almost anything in the way of a house would bring a good rent these days, and especially in this town since it has grown so much. And I never object to adding even a few coppers to my income, especially with three daughters to look after who run up bills all the time. As for Richard, if he doesn't soon get so he can buy himself a car I'm going to have to put my foot down on any more repair bills for my car. By the way, Mona, was it you or Richard who took the sedan out and bent up the rear fender? Why was I not told about it? Really, this business has *got* to stop! We'll all be in the poor house!" Dick Sneller's usually pasty face took on a deep shade of red in his indignation.

His wife felt it wise to step in and smooth matters.

"*I* had the car at the market yesterday, Dick, and when I came out with the groceries I saw the fender. Someone must have bumped it in the parking space."

"Well, why in heaven's name don't you park it where you can watch it and if someone bumps it get their number? I tell you, I can't stand all the expense. We'll just have to give up having a family car."

"Oh, I'll pay for having it fixed. It will come out of the house money!" retorted his wife impatiently. "But for goodness' sake let's get back to this other problem."

"Yes," broke in Mona discontentedly. "Are we really going to have to have that unspeakable western relative here in the way, just as I thought Emory Ames was getting interested in me? She'll likely either be so outlandishly unsophisticated that he'll get a wrong idea of our whole family or else she will be too attractive and get him away from me. Isn't that just life for you?"

"Oh, for cryin' out loud, Mona, can't ya think of anybody but yourself, *ever?*" burst in her twenty-one-year-old brother Richard who was eating with one hand and holding open a tabloid surreptitiously on his knee with the other.

"Keep your mouth shut when you're chewing, brat," was the elder sister's retort. "Dad, isn't your son old enough to know decent manners? I declare, I was so ashamed of the way he carried on at the table the last time Emory was here, I thought I'd perish!"

"If Emory Ames doesn't like our family he can stay away!"

snapped the father. "I'd rather you didn't even *get* married again if it means that your whole family have to live up to the standards of some half-baked fellow who hasn't the grace to keep his thoughts to himself."

Mona flushed with anger and bit her lip. But she knew enough not to answer her father when he was in this mood.

"And as for your western cousin," he went on waving his fork like a policeman's riot stick, "she is certainly to be invited to come here and to stay here as long as she is in this vicinity. You talk about manners. Is it courteous to let your own cousin take a two thousand mile trip to your home town and then have to put up at some miserable little inn? *Of course* she will come here!" He was almost roaring as he finished and even his wife looked at him strangely as he rose from the table and started upstairs.

It was not like Dick to insist upon such hospitality. His son Richard looked after him and then made a grimace at his elder sister.

"Hunh!" he grunted. "I guess you know where to get off now, Mona," he sneered. "I wonder what's struck the old man to take up so for the country cousin all of a sudden." He frowned at the remnants of his apple pie as he tried to think out this new angle.

Mrs. Sneller arose and quickly followed her husband to their room leaving the girls to do the dishes.

"You're right, of course," she began in a placating tone as soon as she entered the room. "I realize that it's the only decent thing to do, but it's certainly *not* convenient for her to come right now." Her voice took on an edge of fretting. "She'll probably be counting on staying at *least* a month. It wouldn't pay her to take the trip for less time than that. But I had planned to have a good bit of company this coming month. There are so *many* social obligations I should pay off. It will make it so much more difficult to have an extra in the house. No guest room, and a crowded table. But I suppose it would look awful if we didn't have her, as she's a real relative."

"Relative be hanged. We'll have to have her, but not for any such fool reason. Listen, Alberta." Dick went stealthily over and closed the door of their room, then he came back to his wife and spoke in a low tone. "You know I've had a lot of heavy expenses lately, and I don't know how I'm going to come out unless I can realize something extra. I had in mind that I could get that house sold before the girl ever saw it and explain to her that there was a large commission to pay because it had involved a good deal of detail in managing the sale. Maybe have some repairs done on it, you know, and charge them up to the estate. After all it's two hundred years old, you remember, and probably could stand some modernizing. It's all in the family, of course, and it's no more than right that we should realize something from old Aunt Agnes' estate after all we have done for her. It would be a sort of evening up of all the care we have given her through the years, you know. If the old soul was so ungrateful as not to leave any of us anything, that is no reason why we should not be repaid out of the estate itself. Now what I have in mind is that we must have the girl here where we can watch her. If she is so blamed independent that she wants to come and see the place, she might take it into her head to try to manage the deal herself and there is no use in simply throwing away what profit we could get out of it. If she were right here under our roof, you can see yourself, she would practically have to follow my advice, and I can manage her much better here. So I want you to write her and invite her to stay here the whole time she is east. Do you understand? Make it imperative so that she can't refuse!"

And Alberta followed his directions so implicitly that when Wynelle received the letter from her cousin she was pleased at the invitation and greatly relieved that the problem of her board while she was away was solved already. Later, if she found she liked the town and wanted to stay she could make other arrangements. How marvelously things were working out for her! She would scarcely need to touch the money that she had saved. It would be enough to keep her for some time in case she had trouble getting a job in Maple Grove. Or just possibly, she thought secretly, she might use it in fixing up the house.

The morning she left to go to the airport she woke early and turned to the little book of verses that she had learned to count on and a smile of wonder lit up her face as she read under the date for that day, "My God shall supply all your need according to His riches in glory by Christ Jesus."

How true that seemed to be for her!

The excitement of going to the airport and actually climbing into the snug little private plane almost made Wynelle forget that she was hired to be a companion for the pleasant little old lady who sat beside her. She fussed over her and tried to think of various little things she could do to make it comfortable and pleasant for her.

But Mrs. Ardsley smiled and waved her off.

"Don't worry about me," she said. "I'm all right. It's just that I didn't want to be without somebody to call on for help if I need it. But I'm not likely to need you. I think we are going to have a splendid trip. Just enjoy yourself, dearie, and wait until I ask you for something."

So Wynelle settled down to watch and take in every detail of the preparations for departure. She admired the confident, skillful way in which the taciturn young pilot went about his work.

"Ed is a fine boy," spoke up her companion when she saw her watching him. "And I hear he is a splendid pilot. We need have no fear of anything going wrong with him at the controls." She gave an assured little smile. "I know quite a bit about him, you know, for he is the son of my best friend, and he married my sister's daughter." She spoke proudly almost as if the young man were her own son, thought Wynelle.

The girl was subconsciously aware of a faint disappointment when Mrs. Ardsley mentioned that the young pilot was married. Then she gave her emotions a little shake. How absurd for her to be thinking so eagerly about every young man she met! This would never do! She was off on her own, and she must keep her head. There would be many young men in the course of her trip, perhaps not all as attractive as this one but she simply could not let herself become even slightly interested in perfect strangers. Ridiculous! Yet a little sigh did escape her. He did seem nice, although she had not as yet exchanged three words with him. Why was it that all the nice ones were already married? She shook her head to get her thoughts on a normal basis again and saw that the pilot was climbing into his seat. She settled back to enjoy to the full the thrill of rising into the air for the first time.

Her lips parted in excitement and her eyes grew wide with delight as she realized that the little toy village she was glimpsing below was old drab, dull Uniontown. To think that she had defeated its monotony at last and was far above it! She almost laughed aloud. She wondered whether all of the circumstances of her life would look as small and insignificant when once she viewed them from Heaven. A feeling of release made her draw a long deep breath and she glanced at little Mrs. Ardsley to see whether she too was experiencing the same thrill in the ride. But the old lady was busy searching for something in her handbag and did not seem to notice that the three of them had already mounted up with wings as eagles.

Wynelle watched eagerly every change of the landscape below her until there was no longer anything that she could identify. Then she bethought her of her charge.

"Are you all right?" she spoke in her ear, for the noise of the plane almost drowned her voice. The old lady nodded with a smile and munched away on some chewing gum she had brought, offering a stick to Wynelle. She took some just to be polite since Mrs. Ardsley seemed to say by gestures that it would be a great help to her, though a help with what, Wynelle could not possibly guess.

The hours sped on and at last when Wynelle had feasted her

fill on the fascinating panorama, she turned her attention to thinking of little things she could do for Mrs. Ardsley. But the little old lady still smiled and shook her head. Wynelle felt very useless so she finally gave up trying and just enjoyed the wonder of the fact that she was really here winging her way to the east coast and a home all her own.

Sometimes she stole a glance at the silent young man ahead of them, wondering if he were always so dour. But watching the sturdy back of his neck and the steady attention he gave to his work she decided that she was glad that there was such a man at the controls.

Wynelle had never beheld such panoramas as she saw spread out below her. The varying patterns of the fields and streams fascinated her, and her beauty-starved eyes appreciated the infinite number of shades and color tones in the landscape. The mountains, like rumpled lengths of green and brown velvet, threaded here and there with a silver river delighted her more than anything else. And when once they rose above a layer of clouds and in every direction as far as she could see there seemed to be heavenly soft snow banks, she was ecstatic. She turned to Mrs. Ardsley with a catch in her breath and her eyes sparkling. The little old lady had been watching her with pleasure, and she smiled back at Wynelle lovingly, thinking how sweet and unspoiled she was, how different from most of the ultra-sophisticated young girls she usually saw.

Wynelle was actually sorry when they finally began to lose altitude and slowly descended to the runway of the Cleveland airport, for that was Mrs. Ardsley's destination. Wynelle had planned to take a train to Washington, spend a day in that city and then go on to Maple Grove which was only about sixty miles from there.

But when the young pilot came to say good-by to his aunt, he gave a glance at Wynelle and noted her bright eager face as she thanked him for her wonderful trip. He allowed himself a flicker of a smile from one corner of his mouth.

"You like flying!" he said.

"Oh, yes!" breathed Wynelle. "I loved it! I was so sorry when you came down! Thank you so much for letting me come along!"

"Where are you headed for?" he asked.

"I'm going on to Washington for a look at our capital," she said eagerly, "then I'm going a little south of there to visit relatives."

He raised his eyebrows.

"I'm taking off for Washington first thing in the morning," he said. "If you want to go along, be out here at the airport at seven."

"Oh!" gasped Wynelle with delight. "Could I? I'd love it! But wouldn't that be imposing on you?"

"Not at all. Be glad to have you," he added impersonally. "I'll look for you at that main entrance there, at seven."

Breathlessly Wynelle thanked him again, and that night she could hardly sleep for thinking of how wonderfully all of her needs had been supplied. Mrs. Ardsley had directed her to a pleasant inexpensive hotel to spend the night and told her how to get out to the airport the next morning.

The sun was pouring its glory over the world when she took up her stand at the entrance gate, watching with interest the ordered activities of the crews, and the coming and going of the great silver birds.

She kept a weather eye out for her pilot, feeling very extra special to think that she was to have a plane and a pilot all her own. Then all at once she saw him walking toward her, waving her on to the far end of the building.

She walked swiftly toward him, trying her best not to seem to be struggling with the weight of her suitcases, for she did not want to be a nuisance. But he noticed her bags and came forward to take them, making some pleasant casual remark about the bright day.

He helped her into the plane and she took the seat she had had the day before. As she climbed aboard she noticed a tall, lean dark-haired young man standing on the ground on the far side of the plane. He was busy with something beneath a wing, and she could not see his face. She supposed he was a mechanic who belonged at the airport. But when at last her pilot climbed in, the other young man followed him and without more than a glance and a nod at her in passing, took the seat beside Ed.

She wondered who he was. He was dressed in a business suit, she noticed now, and did not look like a mechanic. He must be a friend of Ed's, she decided. Both young men treated her quite casually, not discourteously, but simply as if she were a passing stranger. They paid no more attention to her than if she had been a piece of the equipment, not as much, in fact for they seemed to be most particular about everything connected with the plane.

Wynelle studied the back of the new man's head, and decided that he had nice hair, wavy but not too curly, and it was well cut. He had the air of being a gentleman. He held his head very straight and tall; he did not loll as did so many of the young men Wynelle had known at home. When she caught a full view of him she saw that while he was not strikingly handsome, yet there was a noticeable strength of purpose in his face. His lips were set in a firm line and his jaw was clean looking and dependable. She watched him now and again as he turned to Ed and made some remark. She could not hear all that he said. She found herself wishing she could. He spoke little but she saw that Ed seemed to have the greatest respect for anything he said. For a while she found herself building foolish little dreams around him, then as the ship began to climb high once more above the clouds, she shook herself back to normal and enjoyed to the full the splendor of the vastness about them.

They had been flying steadily for some time when Wynelle became aware that the two men were disturbed over something. She glanced out to where they were looking and saw a wiry pencil of black smoke stealing out from beneath the silver wing of their bird. There was alarm in both their faces. A moment more and tongues of orange and crimson and blue appeared. The stranger exchanged a few words with their pilot and then sprang into action. In a few seconds he had the parachute out from above her seat and was undoing the fastenings.

CHAPTER 4

"WE'RE GOING TO have to get out," he said to her in an even voice as if he were telling her that their next stop would be Washington.

"Stand up, please," he ordered courteously. His hands were firm as he deftly placed the belt about her and fastened the buckles. His touch was impersonal and his voice was casual as he said: "When you land you are to stay right where you are until I come or you may get lost. We are not near a town."

In bewilderment Wynelle stood and obeyed his directions.

"Take your money and stuff it inside your dress," he told her. "We'll not be able to save anything." Her hands were shaking as she obeyed. He gave her a swift keen look but she forced a smile and tried to seem as calm as he. A gleam of admiration came and went in his face but he said nothing.

Before she was scarcely aware of what was happening, he had stood her with her back to the side wall of the plane and he was facing her. And now he hesitated, looking at her gravely, searchingly, as if he were actually seeing her for the first time, as if she were a real person and not simply a piece of cargo.

He looked straight into her eyes, his hands on her shoulders checking once more the straps of her harness. Her wide eyes gazed back at him, struggling to hide her terror. Then he spoke.

"Are you born again?" he asked abruptly.

Wynelle stammered in bewilderment.

"I mean," he added speaking fast, "are you saved? Are you a Christian?" He spoke more gently this time but still in a tense voice as if time were slipping fast, and what he had to say was vital.

"Oh!" she gasped. "Why, yes—yes, I guess so." She felt a little shiver of shame that she had not yet thought in this extremity to call upon God.

"You've got to *know!* Are you trusting Jesus Christ as your Saviour?" he demanded. He spoke insistently as if it were a matter of life and death.

"Yes," she answered more firmly.

For the first time since she had met him he relaxed for an instant from his grimness and almost smiled. It was as if a light glowed within him somewhere. She was astonished at the radiance of his face.

"Okay, then *pray!*" he ordered.

A sudden terrible trembling seized her.

"You are frightened, of course," he added gently, holding her arms in a comforting grasp. "But don't worry. You and I are going to take a little side trip together!" he smiled. "It won't take long and it's the only way. Hold tight to me," he instructed. He grinned again, gaily, as if they were about to start off on a roller coaster ride in an amusement park,

Wynelle had turned wide eyes of alarm up to his when he first spoke, but there was such assurance in his smile that she thought now that she must surely have been mistaken in thinking there was danger. This must be merely some sort of life-saving practice, like the fire drills they used to have at school.

The young man put one arm firmly about her waist and reached behind her with the other. Suddenly there was a wrenching sound and a gust of wind took her breath away. Then Wynelle felt herself pushed out into space.

There was a horrible drop into emptiness. All the life seemed to be sucked out of her. All she knew was that strong arms were about her. The noise of the airplane faded away and there was only the swishing of air to be heard. It seemed as if she had suddenly been transported to another world.

All at once a violent jerk tore her from the man's grasp and there was a loud clap like thunder. She swung wildly back and forth in wide gyrations. Then gently she began to glide toward the earth. The pit of her stomach found its right place again after being up in her throat somewhere.

But something was gone. That wonderful reassuring smile was no longer there, and the arms were no longer about her. She had so nearly lost her senses in that first fierce plunge that she could scarcely understand what had happened. One instant she had been aware of the stranger face to face with her, then the next moment she found herself alone between earth and sky. Had the man lost his hold and fallen? How terrible! She tried to look down to see but the awful height sickened her and she had to close her eyes again. Her heart was pounding so that she thought there was nothing in her body but her heart.

Gradually she gained courage to open her eyes once more. She saw the tops of trees coming swiftly up to meet her and she closed them again. Then something seemed to tear at her side and her arm and she came to a sudden stop with a jerk that almost snapped her neck.

Wondering whether she were actually dead or alive, she dared to open her eyes again and found that she was dangling by the ropes of her parachute which were caught in the limbs of a tree. The branches had scraped her as she fell and torn her dress and bruised her so that the blood was flowing. She was scarcely aware of being hurt, however, and she closed her eyes again as a faintness stole over her. It was several minutes before she could take a long deep breath and look about to see what she should do.

She was not more than six feet above the ground, and she was held securely by the straps of her harness. But it was a most uncomfortable position. She felt like a turtle, with arms and legs sprawling. She had a sudden desire to laugh at herself. The whole thing had taken such a few moments that it still seemed like a dream. Not five minutes ago she had been sitting quietly in the plane enjoying the ride. Now here she was hung in a tree a hundred miles, perhaps, from anywhere.

As her senses returned to her clearly she began to wonder what had become of the young man who had jumped with her. And where was the plane and its pilot? Perhaps they were both in trouble and she was the only one who knew about the accident. She wondered whether the stranger had had a parachute too, or whether in his calm courage he had given her the only one there was. Surely a plane would be required to carry enough chutes for the passengers! But how wonderful he had been in his thoughtfulness for her. He had accomplished the escape so skillfully and so quickly that she had had little time to work up a fright. As she thought over all that he had done she realized that his first thought must have been for her, and her heart filled with amazement and gratitude.

She had no silly illusions about him. The whole thing had been far too serious for that. It had been a matter of life and death and he had considered her life first. It thrilled her to think that there was a man like that in the world. She suddenly felt as if she must go to him and thank him right away. She struggled to turn and see how she might free herself.

She reached back as far as she could but she was not quite able to grasp the rope that held her suspended. She even kicked her feet back trying to catch her toe in the rope. But it evaded her every time. How long would she have to hang there? Would the stranger who had rescued her once, ever find her in this waste land?

There was nothing to be seen in any direction but scrub pines and dreary wilderness. She tried to raise her head enough to look off at a distance but it strained her neck and she had to give it up.

Perhaps the man was not far off and was trying to find her. If she called out that might help him, so she shouted.

"Here! Here I am!"

But her voice sounded so small in the vast loneliness that it made her shudder. And after calling several times she found that her breath was gone, for the straps were too tight around her to be comfortable.

The wallet that she had stuffed in the neck of her dress was pressing against her sharply. At least that told her that she still had it. But what good would her precious three hundred dollars do her out here?

A long time she hung there, moving as little as possible for she soon found that every move only made the straps cut into her flesh more sharply.

Now and then the horrid thought that the brave young man who had helped her had been killed himself crept up and stole into the dark corners of her mind. Again and again she shut it out but she knew that it would return and it did. Finally it dared to come right out and look her in the face. It said: "Suppose both the men have been killed! If they are who would know to look for another passenger? Perhaps no one saw the parachute come down. When will anyone ever happen out this wild way?"

Terror began to take hold of her, and a trembling seized her again. She must get down. She *must*. Again she struggled and twisted. Time and again she thought she was about to reach the ropes to pull herself up, but she couldn't quite make it. Exhausted she sank limply against her harness again.

She thought several hours must have gone by. Again the fear for her stranger rescuer tortured her. She tried to recall whether she had seen him strap a chute on himself, as he stood talking so calmly to her, but all she could remember was the steady glow of his eyes as he had bid her, "Pray."

Pray! Why hadn't she? She had been too excited. Well, she was safe now, comparatively so. Perhaps he had prayed for her; he had had to do everything else for her! Suddenly forgetting her own plight she cried aloud, "Oh God! save that man! He mustn't be killed because of me. Get me down from here so that I can find him!" Over and over she said it, and the tears rained down her face in her earnestness. If only she were free she could search for him. She decided to try once more to see if she couldn't reach the rope above her. And just then a rustling in a tree nearby caused her to look up and there was a squirrel swinging on the tip end of a long limb. The branch gave with him and he jumped. All at once she realized that if only she could get to swinging back and forth, perhaps that would carry her far enough to reach another branch. So she started to rock back and forth gently, taking advantage of each increase in her swing until at last she was describing quite an arc in the air. There was another branch not far away. If she could grasp it, she could pull herself up far enough, perhaps, so that the weight on the straps would be eased and then she could undo her buckles. Back and forth, back and forth she swung, wishing she had spent some of her years in a circus! At last she thought she could make it on the next forward swing. Timing her reach carefully, she seized a small branch near the end of the large one. But her weight was such that on the downswing the little twig snapped and she was flung back again, all out of rhythm now. Her heart sank. But after she had got her breath from the shaking it gave her she decided that if she could swing far enough to reach that small branch she could probably work herself a little farther next time and grasp the large one. So, in spite of her sore muscles and her bruises, she started her swing again. And this time she made it. The pull on her hands was cruel, but she held on and pulled until she managed to get one arm over the limb. Painfully she worked until she got her buckles loosened and then she dropped, utterly worn out, onto the soft ground below the tree.

She lay there for several minutes, getting her breath and rubbing the sore spots on her body. But as time went on she began to be more frightened for the young man than for herself. He might be in far worse case than she. She had thought over every detail of what had taken place and she realized now that he must have stayed with her long enough to pull her rip cord, and then dropped farther himself so as not to entangle her with his chute. Perhaps he had fallen too far for his chute to open. Or perhaps something had gone wrong with it. She remembered his command to stay where she was until he should come, but she felt as if she must make some effort to find him before dark. She struggled to her feet and called again. Without the straps that had bound her she could shout louder. Four or five times she called and listened. But there was no sound except the little rustlings of small wood folk.

Wildly she gazed about her. There was no sign of human life anywhere. No farmhouse with a friendly banner of smoke from its chimney. So at last with a pounding heart she started off through the brush.

Every step she took was painful for she had received some really bad bruises in her fall into the tree, but all she could think of was that the stranger who had risked his life for her, might be needing help. She kept seeing his clear kind eyes facing hers, and hearing his voice say, "Okay, then pray!"

The words comforted her. She knew that a man who believed in prayer would be praying too, if he were alive, perhaps for her as well as himself. And suddenly she realized that the prayer she had offered while she hung from the tree had been answered! She was down and free, yet she had forgotten even to say thank you for her deliverance!

"Oh Lord, I'm an ungrateful thing. You did help me, didn't You! Thank You. And now I want to ask something again. I don't deserve that You should do anything for me, but if that young man is out here somewhere needing help, won't You let me find him, please? Or You take care of him somehow?"

The tears were streaming down Wynelle's face now, and she was fairly running over the rough ground.

"Where are you? Oh, yoohoo! Where are you?" she kept crying breathlessly. Still there was no answer.

The sun sank lower and lower. Its long straight fingers reached through the branches of trees above her and seemed to point at her in mockery.

She had selected at random a direction in which to walk which she thought was due east. She reasoned that there would, of necessity be less distance to go east than west. East would eventually bring her to the ocean with beach cottages if she kept on long enough. Surely there would be some dwelling, somewhere, before long.

It was quite dark and the moon was coming up when, struggling through swampy ground, she thought she saw the squared corners of something built by man. Breathless, almost exhausted, she hurried on toward it.

It proved to be a tiny fisher's hut, long abandoned. It was on the edge of a narrow winding river. Wynelle shivered and stopped, fearful lest there might be some wild man of the woods in there. Yet it was entirely dark, and there was no sign of life.

It was growing cold; at least the four flimsy walls would shelter her for the night. She circled the little house carefully before she dared cross the threshold. At last she entered screwing up her courage to duck under an enormous spider web, silvery in the moonlight, at the top of the doorway.

There was absolutely nothing in the house, not even a stray board for a pillow. Weary and half sick, Wynelle dropped down on the dusty bare floor, too worn out to care about the dirt or the hardness of the old boards.

As she dropped off to sleep the thought of her empty bed back in Uniontown came to her. It seemed so soft and clean and desirable at this distance. She gave a groan. Was this the way the prodigal son had felt when he was off in the far country? She gave a twisted smile at herself. Had she been wrong, perhaps, to wish to change the lot that God had chosen for her? Was this His way to show her that there would be trouble everywhere except in the one place that He wanted her? She was too tired to think that out, but she sighed a weary little prayer as she fell asleep!

"Oh, God, if I've done wrong in coming away, I'm sorry. But now that I'm in this jam, will You please get me out of it, because I can't help myself, You know that. And please take care of that wonderful guy that helped me."

A bat stirred and flew out of a broken pane of the window; a little field mouse hurried across the floor to see who his strange visitor was, but Wynelle slept on trustingly, her head on her arm, the other hand grasping firmly the wallet in her dress.

CHAPTER 5

THE NEXT MORNING Wynelle awoke to so many bruises and sore muscles that she felt she could not move. But it was out of the question for her to spend any more time in this miserable hut. She would die of starvation if not of fear. She had had nothing to eat since breakfast yesterday except some berries she had found by the way.

She forced herself to stand up and make her way to the little river. It looked so bright and sparkling that she was tempted to drink, but she knew that was risky, so she contented herself with a good thorough wash to her face and hands, and then she wet her lips and tongue. She started bravely off along the river, feeling sure that in time such a gay little stream would have some human beings attracted to its banks. Several times during the morning she was so weary that she sank down beside the water and struggled with the tears. Then she reminded herself that tears would certainly never get her anywhere, and she got up and went on.

At last about noon, she rounded a bend in the river and came upon a little village which looked like a summer camp. It could not be called a resort, for the little houses were mere huts, and the few people she saw were dressed more like farmers or fishermen than like folk who were off on a vacation. But they were human beings and she was glad. As she trudged up the one little street she suddenly became aware of her appearance. She knew that she had probably not cleansed her face very thoroughly in spite of her energetic efforts; and she had had no mirror to show her how very soiled it was, no comb to smooth her hair. Her pretty dark blue faille suit was torn in a long gash down one side and even her slip hung in tatters. Her blouse was torn too and grimy from her night in the cabin. Looking like this, perhaps nobody would help her.

With a flutter of apprehension she approached a tall gaunt man in dungarees and hip boots who had a fishing pole over his shoulder. She tried to hold shut the tear in her skirt, and smooth back her hair with the other hand. She had a feeling that he might look her over and walk away.

But as she looked up at him she saw that his eyes were kindly. He seemed to pay no attention to her garb.

"Would you please tell me what town this is," she asked. "And how I could get to Washington?"

The man removed his pipe and spit.

"Ain't no town, I reckon," he responded. "Town's six mile futher up the river. Name o' Pippinville. It ain't much of a town, neither. Whar youall from?"

The girl laughed.

"From up in the air, really," she said. "We had to jump from our plane yesterday. It was on fire. And I landed in a tree somewhere down there!" She pointed in the direction from which she had come.

"Wall, I swan!" The man spit again. "I swan!" he repeated. "Bill!" he called to a man who was just coming out of the one little store in the place. "This yere gal lit yestiddy from that plane we saw. I sez to Bill," he went on turning back to Wynelle, "I sez I was sure somep'n was wrong with thet thar. It was actin' up thet strange!"

"Oh," cried Wynelle, "do you know where it came down? I have been so worried lest the pilot was killed. There was another man, too, who jumped with me, and I haven't been able to find him. Would there be any way to search for him? I was so tired I couldn't go any farther—I—" Suddenly Wynelle sank down in a heap on the ground at the feet of the two fishermen.

"I swan!" ejaculated the tall one. "Must be plumb wore out. Bill, git some water. I'll go call my wife."

In a few minutes the whole little village was waiting upon Wynelle, and slowly she opened her eyes and looked around her, remembering where she was.

"Oh!" she exclaimed apologetically. "I'm sorry to have made you all so much trouble. I must have passed out." She gave a weak little giggle. "I guess I'm just hungry." The effort of speaking made her head swim again and she closed her eyes once more, much to the consternation of the tall man who thought surely she would faint again.

He leaned down and picked her up in his arms and with a command: "Git her some vittles, ma," he marched off to his own cabin across the street.

Later that day, washed and mended and combed, well fed by Ma Simpson, and driven in state by her tall new friend, Wynelle rode in his jeep into the town of Pippinville.

There they bought a Washington paper and discovered that a plane had crashed the day before, and its pilot had been taken to the hospital in a nearby city. An unidentified man had been found unconscious, with his parachute still fastened on him, and had also been taken to the hospital. But the name of the hospital was not given. The paper said that the condition of the men was hopeful.

Wynelle puzzled over what to do. She felt as if she ought to hunt up her fellow flyers at least, and thank them for saving her life. But she had no information to go on. She couldn't travel from hospital to hospital asking for a patient named Ed. And she had no idea what the stranger's name was.

At last she decided that the best she could do was to go on to her own destination and write back to the little old lady Mrs. Ardsley, at her Uniontown address. The letter would be forwarded. And she would enclose a note to be sent on to Ed and the stranger, expressing as well as she could her thanks and wishing them a swift recovery. It seemed a poor way to show her gratitude, but it was all she could do now.

So she thanked her tall fisherman and said good-by, sending with him a big box of candy for his wife and three little boys, and then as it was late in the afternoon, she hurried to Pippinville's general store and bought herself a cheap little pasteboard overnight bag, lest when she got to the city she would not be accepted for lodging without some baggage.

She stowed a few necessities in it, putting off buying much because she knew that she must save her money. There was no telling what expenses she would have to meet before she reached her cousins.

The bus driver who took her to the city directed her to a fairly good tourist home, with a clean soft bed that invited sleep. She sent a telegram to her cousins telling them that she was delayed and would arrive the next evening. Then with a thankful heart she went to sleep and dreamed that she was still wandering through underbrush, calling for the man whose name she did not know. By this time he had begun to seem like a hero in a story book. Well, she had left home to have some adventures, and she was certainly having them!

But the telegram started another furor in the Sneller household.

"Oh, heck, mom," stormed Mona flinging the telegram down on the dining room table for her mother to pick up for herself and read. "This means that the dope will turn up just about the time Emory Ames does. What a mess. And dad will fuss, I suppose, if I don't give up everything and get down on my knees to her. What strange fancy has taken him to be so nice to just a relative, I don't know!"

Mrs. Sneller took the telegram and as she read a frown creased her large forehead.

"The worst is that I'll have to get up another company dinner, I suppose, for her first night here. Most of what we were going to have tonight won't keep over. If only your father wouldn't act so perfectly ridiculous about treating this cousin as if she were a queen!" Then Mrs. Sneller checked herself. "Oh, well, I guess it can't be helped. It's better to be nice to her. You may find that you will like her very much, Mona."

"*Like* her!" screamed Mona, taking out her bobby pins so that her short hair stood out like springs all over her head. "I wouldn't like her if she was a princess. She's upsetting all my plans. I just know she will be a pain in the neck. I'm telling you," Mona's bulgy eyes glared right into her mother's face, "if she tries to steal Emory Ames from me, I'll *kill* her!"

"Oh Mona," remonstrated her mother, "don't take on so. For pity's sake don't make a scene; at least until your father can get the business end of things settled up."

"Oh-h?" sneered Mona with a rising inflection designed to irritate. "I *thought* there was some ulterior motive in dad's sudden courtesy! Okay, I'll be decent, but I can't last long."

The next afternoon on the ride out to Maple Grove, Wynelle spent some time wondering what her new cousins would be like. From Alberta's cordial letter she had decided that she would probably be very friendly and perhaps motherly in a way. She gave a little wistful sigh. Her recent experiences had made her feel so much more alone and friendless than she had since she left home. There being six cousins, Wynelle had pictured a jolly happy family. It would be good to be with loving relatives again.

Judging from his letter, Dick Sneller, she had thought, would be brusque and business-like. He might be a little portly, for he and his wife must be middle-aged to have a daughter who was already married and divorced. That daughter was a problem in Wynelle's mind. She wondered what terrible thing her young husband had done that she could have been willing to cast him off once she had taken him into her heart. Wynelle's early training had been strict on the matter of faithfulness in marriage and she considered divorce as something to be resorted to only in the most extreme

circumstances. Before she arrived at Maple Grove she was already
picturing the Snellers' eldest daughter as a fragile wisp of a girl
who had been terribly abused and was heartbroken. The boy and
the other two girls she knew nothing about. It might be nice, she
thought, to have a boy cousin near her own age. She had always
wished for a brother.

So when she arrived, in a trim brown and white cotton dress
she had found on a bargain rack in Washington, with a natty
little white piqué cap on her head, she was all smiles and eagerness.

She was just a bit dashed to find nobody at the bus station to
meet her. She had told them what time her bus would get in, so
that they would know whether to count on her for dinner or not.
Well, that was all right, perhaps they had some engagement that
had kept them from meeting her. Or perhaps something was
wrong with their car. It was possible that they had no car, although
Wynelle had always understood that her cousins were fairly well-
to-do.

So Wynelle walked, much relieved to discover that the Sneller
house was only eight blocks from the station. She smiled wryly
to herself as she thought of the miles she had traversed through the
underbrush two days before. Eight blocks seemed very short compared to that trek. As always when the thought of the airplane
came to her mind, she wondered again how the two young men
were. Well, perhaps her cousin Dick would be able to locate them
for her.

The Sneller house was on the main street of Maple Grove, which
at first sight seemed not a pretty but a proper little town. Its build-
ings were in good repair. They were not modern, but on the other
hand they were not shabby. They wore their shiny coats of paint
over their old wooden frames with pride. The streets seemed to
be full of brisk, busy people. The whole town gave the impression
that it was fairly bursting with respectable citizens. Wynelle's
eyes glanced interestedly around, trying to guess whether any of

the small houses she could see might be her own. No, she recalled that her mother had said that Grandmother Williams had insisted on buying farther out, on the edge of town.

The sun was hot and Wynelle was glad that she had only the small bag to carry. When she arrived at the Sneller house she felt a little stirring of disappointment. It was a drab yellowish-brown frame with a high peak in front above a steep porch roof. It had the air of looking down its nose over a very high collar. Wynelle hoped that the house did not give indication of the kind of people who lived within its doors.

She rang the old-fashioned bell and after a few moments a colored girl came to the door and looked at her.

"I think Mrs. Sneller was expecting me," she said brightly. "I am her cousin."

"Oh," responded the servant. "You can come in. She said for you to make yourself at home till she gets here. This is her bridge club day and she don't never get home till after five. Come this-away. You're to be in Mis' Mona's room."

The living room was long and narrow, across the front of the house. It was furnished in heavy dark walnut upholstered with rather colorless cotton tapestry. The girl led Wynelle across the room and through a hallway and stopped before a door that stood ajar.

"Miss Mona," the maid raised her voice a little, "here's yer comp'ny."

She gave the door a little shove and nodding to Wynelle to enter she went back to her duties in the kitchen.

Rather taken aback, Wynelle took a hesitant step, and heard an unhappy voice say,

"Okay. You can come in."

Trying to summon a smile, Wynelle stepped into a small cluttered room, too full of furniture, and saw a girl who she thought must be years older than herself, half reclining on a soiled chaise longue. She was putting her hair up in pin curls and they did not become her, for her forehead bulged. A movie magazine was in her lap and a chocolate bar half eaten on the floor beside her.

She took a swift glance at Wynelle, a glance which did not miss her worn shoes.

"H'warya?" She asked the question as if she had decided in that length of time that it did not matter much how this new cousin was. "Pardon *me* for not getting up. I was afraid I'd drop all these pins. 'Dja have a good trip?" She was obviously trying hard to be what she would call polite.

"Well, it was interesting," laughed Wynelle taking a seat on the disheveled bed, "although it was quite—different!"

Mona looked up with a spark of interest.

"How nice. Nothing much is different any more. No thrills!" She spoke in a bitter disillusioned tone.

"This was, definitely!" Wynelle laughed again vivaciously. "I never hope to have any greater thrill. Our plane caught fire and we had to jump."

"Oh my gosh!" exclaimed Mona. "You don't mean it. Weren't you scared simply stiff! I'd die before I ever got to the ground, I know!"

"I guess I didn't have much time to get scared," Wynelle answered. "The only passenger besides the pilot buckled me up and pushed me out before I scarcely knew what was going on. He was wonderful. But—" She looked troubled. "I'm still not sure whether he came out of it all right."

"He!" Mona caught her up. "A man in the scene, eh? Tall dark and handsome?"

Wynelle smiled, but somehow she resented this strange girl. It seemed as if she had no right even to talk about the wonderful stranger who had been so careful of her and had risked his life to save her.

"Yes, he was tall," she said slowly, "very tall, and dark. I don't know that you'd call him handsome. He looked—*good* and dependable."

"Oh how gruesome!" ejaculated Mona. "Heaven preserve me from such! Still, any man is a relief at times!"

Wynelle's heart sank. Was she to have to share a room with this unattractive cousin? The prospective length of her visit began to shrink in her mind.

"You can put your things in the closet if you want. I hope you don't have much, because it's rather crowded already. This used to be a breakfast room and my brother had it before I got married, but when I came back here he had moved up to my room and wouldn't change, so I'm stuck with it. Mercy, is that the only suitcase you have? Where is your other baggage?"

Wynelle gasped a little and then laughed.

"I wish I knew," she said ruefully.

"What's the matter? Did it get lost coming east? I hope it gets here soon, because I can't lend you anything much. I have few enough things as it is."

"Not exactly lost," said Wynelle. "I suppose it's burned up. I had to leave everything in the plane when we jumped."

"You mean you really did such a crazy thing?" questioned Mona unbelievingly. "I thought you must have made all that up to make an impression."

The red flamed up in Wynelle's face, and she had to struggle to keep her temper. "I do like to fool sometimes," she finally admitted, "but I hardly think it would have been a suitable time to lie, do you? When I was meeting you for the first time?"

Mona only shrugged.

Wynelle was glad to hear the front screen door open just then and heavy footsteps go into the kitchen a moment. Perhaps that was her cousin Alberta. She might prove to be less prickly than her daughter. Perhaps it was because the poor girl had been through so much that she was ready to distrust everybody.

Wynelle had just about recovered her equilibrium, although

neither girl had spoken again, when Mrs. Sneller came into the room.

"Oh, you found your room all right, did you?" she said to Wynelle in a preoccupied tone. "I hope you didn't mind my not being here to welcome you at first. It was *unavoidable*. Did you have a good trip?"

Wynelle was opening her mouth to answer when Mona spoke up.

"She gave me some tale about having to parachute down!" she told her mother. "I really didn't know whether to believe her or not."

"*Really?*" exclaimed Mrs. Sneller. "Mercy *me,* what an experience! You must tell us all about it. But I *must* go now and dress for dinner. Perhaps you will have a chance to describe it all to everyone at the table. I'm sure my son would be most interested to hear it. We're having just a simple little dinner tonight. Don't bother to dress much. Mona, show her where everything is, won't you?"

Mrs. Sneller hurried out before Wynelle had a chance to tell her that the dress she had on was absolutely all she owned except the torn faille suit which she had stowed away in her bag to be mended carefully at her leisure.

She looked down at her dress, troubled.

"What are you going to wear tonight, Mona?"

"Oh, I suppose I'll be wearing my only decent dinner dress," grumbled Mona. "It's that red rag with the taffeta puffed sleeves hanging there in the closet. But you don't need to dress that much. I have a date tonight." She giggled self-consciously.

"Well, it's really not a question of what I *should* wear," Wynelle said with an attempt to be gay. "I don't have another thing but this that I have on. Will it do? I don't want to disgrace you all." She said it wistfully.

Mona shrugged again.

"It doesn't matter. But you can put on that old blue silk of mine if you want. I guess mom will like it better if you're dressed up. You can say that your baggage hasn't come yet, you know."

Much as she disliked the idea, Wynelle hesitantly slid out of her dainty little chambray and tried on Mona's blue silk. As it went over her head she gave a little shudder. It smelled of old perfume and perspiration and cleaning fluid mixed together. She was very much relieved to find that it was far too large for her. Mona insisted that she could wear one of her big sashes to hold it in, but Wynelle finally put her foot down.

"If I must explain anyway that my things haven't come, what difference does it make what I have on? If you don't mind I think I'll just wear my own dress, please."

Mona gave a shrug and marched off to the bathroom to get herself ready.

As soon as she was out of the room Wynelle sank down on the edge of the double bed and gazed around forlornly. What a place! Soiled garments lay where they had fallen; one nylon stocking was draped over the footboard the other sprawled out from under the bed, with a roll of dust enmeshed in it and a gaudy platform slipper upside down upon it. The closet door stood open and it seemed like a chamber of horrors to the tired lonely girl. The bedspread had been pretty once but it was smeared here and there with lipstick and it was hanging long at one end and short at the other. The dresser was jammed with bottles of cosmetics and the scarf looked as if it had not been changed for weeks. A dark brown hole had been burned in it by a cigarette. One drawer was open, showing a mass of all sorts of clothing that Mona apparently had just been rummaging through.

Altogether, the picture was discouraging. Evidently the visiting of relatives, especially unknown ones, was not all that it had seemed to be from the vantage point of Uniontown. Wynelle heaved a sigh. As her mother had said, probably she had been crazy to come on this trip at all. Her experience two days ago would certainly indicate that she was not to expect an easy time.

Was God trying to show her something by all this? She had no very deep knowledge of His ways, but she had always been taught that a child of His could depend on Him to teach whatever needed to be learned. In a vague general way she had always considered herself submissive to His training. But what could He possibly teach her in this place? This girl was actually repulsive to her. How could two people who were related by blood, even distantly, be so utterly different from each other? Well, perhaps she was judging too soon. There must be some pleasant qualities in the girl. And she had yet to meet the other members of the family. She took a deep breath and arose to comb her hair and do what she could to make herself presentable for dinner.

CHAPTER 6

Roger Blackstone stirred and groaned. It seemed to him as if he had been surrounded for an eternity by a steel band which was closing in on his head. Sometimes the steel was blue and cold. Other times it seemed red hot. He thought the band had been there for weeks or perhaps months. Up until the last few minutes he had been powerless against it. Now he was almost sure that if he could only open his eyes that would break the band. He had tried several times. He exerted all his will power and finally forced them to open.

The steel band was not released. It was still there, but now he knew what it was, a terrible aching in his head. He saw gray walls, and a girl with a white cap on. He must be sick! His eyes fell shut again but he began to think. The effort made the steel band tighter, but he groped for facts and at last he remembered the plane ride and the flames. Once more he opened his eyes and saw the nurse. She was smiling. He could feel her finger on his wrist. He tried to speak but she stopped him.

"You're feeling better!" she told him. "But you are to lie quiet now, and I'll bring you something to eat."

He faded out of consciousness, more out of physical weakness than from submission, but it was not for long. When the nurse returned he was awake.

"What happened to the plane?" he asked abruptly in a weak voice. "Does anybody know? The pilot was a friend of mine."

"Yes, the pilot's all right. He's going to get well. He's here in the hospital and when you are better you may go in to see him."

"What happened? I can't seem to remember it all. I fell, didn't I?"

"You had a parachute on when they picked you up," she told him.

"Wasn't there somebody else in the plane?" he asked in a troubled voice.

"Apparently there was nobody but you and the pilot."

Suddenly he pushed her hand away with the spoonful of soup she was feeding him and tried to sit up.

"Yes, there was! A girl. I fastened a chute on her and we jumped. Hasn't she been found? I told her to stay where she was until I came." He was excited now and the nurse hastily put down the spoon and tried to calm him.

"You must be quiet, sir," she insisted. "You have had a bad fall and you have concussion. You *must* not get yourself worked up over anything."

"But the girl may be out in that wilderness all alone. Good heavens! Perhaps she's dead, or in pain. Tell me, nurse, how long have I been here?"

"They picked you up and brought you in two days ago. Now you must lie still or I will have to call the doctor!"

"Well, call him then!" retorted Roger. "I'm not going to lie here in pink cotton and leave that kid out in the wilds to die."

"I will report it, sir, and you may just put it out of your mind. It will be taken care of."

"Okay, but I want you to come back here and tell me just what you do about it!" commanded Roger. "Just as soon as you can. If you don't I'm going to get up and get out of here."

"I'll be sure to tell you. Now *please* lie still!" repeated the nurse.

His head aching worse than ever, Roger lay back on his pillow but he could not close his eyes. He kept seeing before him the sweet face of the girl who had trusted him so bravely. What a soldier she had been! No screaming or carrying on. She had simply obeyed orders. What if she had obeyed to the extent of remaining in the spot where she alighted? What if she had a broken leg or something, and was suffering out there all alone?

Roger had worked himself up into a fever by the time the nurse came back to tell him that a search party would start out immediately. They would keep him informed of any progress. He had to be content with that, but he secretly determined that he would be well enough to go out himself the next day, if there was no news of the girl.

All that day he kept his nurse busy calling one source of information after another, seeking for some word of her. He insisted on calling the newspaper office of every town within twenty-five miles of the spot where the plane had crashed. But Pippinville had no newspaper of its own, so no news of the strange girl who had passed through came to him.

He begged to be allowed to speak to his friend Ed, but they told him that although Ed was conscious the doctor had forbidden any reference to the crash for another day or two.

So Roger was forced to lie back and wait with as much patience as he could muster.

About that time the dinner gong sounded in the Sneller household. With apprehension Wynelle sought the dining room. Mona said, "Go on or dad'll have kittens. I'll be there in a jerk. My boy friend is likely to turn up any time and I've got to be ready."

So, all unescorted, Wynelle entered the room where the head of the house was already rubbing his hands and frowning around to see which ones were missing from their seats.

Alberta spoke up, quite as if she had forgotten Wynelle's presence in the house, and said, "Oh! This is Wynelle, our cousin from out west, Dick."

Mr. Sneller arose from his chair and bowed.

Mrs. Sneller named over her children to Wynelle, but before she had finished Mr. Sneller was back in his seat saying crossly,

"Can't we eat now? I've got to go out to that board meeting tonight. We can't stand around all evening."

Feeling very much out of place Wynelle slipped into the chair

Mrs. Sneller indicated and looked toward the head of the table, wondering whether Mr. Sneller would give thanks for the food. But he was already deep in his meat loaf, pausing only to say, "How was your trip?"

Wynelle had already learned that her exciting adventure did not seem so interesting to others as to herself, so she merely answered,

"Oh it was beautiful! I just loved the flight. I had never been up before and I enjoyed every minute of it."

Mr. Sneller looked up in disapproval.

"You mean you flew! Wasn't that rather expensive?"

Wynelle flushed.

"Why no," she said. "My brother-in-law arranged for me to accompany a friend of his on a private flight nearly all the way. It was wonderful!"

"Oh!" spoke up Mrs. Sneller. "It *that* why you had an accident? I shouldn't care to trust myself to these little private planes. The pilots are *bound* to be less experienced than those in the big air-lines."

"Accident!" put in Richard Jr., with interest. "Did you have an accident? Much thrill?"

Wynelle smiled and took a second look at him. She had not been greatly impressed with him at first. He was fairly tall but pale, with straw-colored straight hair and a little strawlike mustache.

His eyes were set rather too close together, but they had a friendly light in them, and Wynelle had a feeling that perhaps not every person here was ready to pounce upon everything she said and discount it.

"Yes, quite," she answered, ready to make gay conversation of her recent harrowing experience if that would ease the tension of the atmosphere. "The plane caught fire and we had to jump. I never rode in a parachute before and while the first mile or so is a little breath-taking, the rest was most fascinating. 'Never a dull moment.' " She laughed with a musical lilt.

Richard Jr. laid down his fork and seized upon the new cousin as it were, with a gleam of pleasure.

"What a gal!" he exclaimed. "Where have you been all my life?" He gave her an admiring stare. Wynelle felt like drawing back from his look, but it was such a relief to have someone really pleasant to her that she controlled her distaste and threw him a comradely smile.

Just then Mona made her appearance and her father interrupted the conversation to storm at her tardiness. When she had flippantly returned his sharp thrusts and taken her seat, Della, the next younger sister, went back to the subject of the accident.

"Too bad there wasn't a tall dark and handsome hero to rescue you," she giggled. Della was sixteen, and pretty in a rather coarse way. She scented romance in everything.

"As a matter of fact," answered Wynelle innocently, "there was!"

"Oh!" squealed Della. "Where have you hidden him?"

Wynelle looked troubled. "I wish I knew," she said. "I hope he's in a hospital in a town not far from Washington, but I don't know how badly he is hurt. He jumped with me and pulled my cord and then I never saw him again."

"My word!" exclaimed Della. "Maybe he's dead!"

Wynelle winced. "I sincerely hope not!" she said quietly. "There was a notice in the Washington paper about a plane crash in which two young men were hurt, but their names were not given. I wouldn't have known his name anyway."

"You mean you flew all the way from Kansas with him and never found out his *name?* How you do waste opportunities!" She stared at Wynelle as if she were a strange specimen.

Mr. Sneller changed the subject then, discussing with his wife some arrangements about the week end, and Wynelle was glad to have the spotlight shifted from herself.

All this time the fourteen-year-old daughter, Thelma, had gazed at her solemnly from time to time through her large modernistic

tortoise shell glasses. Her look held neither smile, nor sneer.
Wynelle could not make her out. It seemed that there were three
classes of people, those you were drawn to, those you shrank from,
and those who were just a blank. Wynelle shrank from most of
this family, unless it might be Richard who had appeared to be
friendly. But this Thelma child seemed to be a blank.

In her lonely heart Wynelle remembered the comforting arms
of that stranger who had held her so safely. How she wished
for such a refuge now. She shuddered at the unfriendliness here.
In contrast her friend of the plane seemed like an ally. Where
was he now? Was he as lonely as she? Probably not. Very likely
by this time he had a loving family about him ministering to his
needs. She wished she could do something for him but she supposed that she would be utterly unnecessary in the picture. She
wrenched her thoughts back to the Snellers.

Thelma was tall for her age, and gangling. She had a ponderous-
looking book thrust behind her in her chair. Wynelle discovered
later that she always carried one with her to give the impression
that she was intellectual. "I plan to study medicine," she explained one day to Wynelle, "specializing in psychognosy." The
long words seemed ridiculous coming from such a childish looking creature.

Thelma had subjected Wynelle to her scrutiny ever since dinner had started. Now she heaved an obvious sigh as if she had
classified her at last.

Della glanced at her younger sister with scorn.

"Mother," she appealed to higher authority, "for pity's sake
stop Thelma from staring so. It's positively rude."

Thelma turned her pallid gaze on Della and remarked in a flat
disillusioned voice, "Strange, how it is only the human animal
that resents curiosity."

But Mrs. Sneller looked indulgently at her youngest daughter.
"Oh, I guess everybody knows she doesn't mean any harm by
it, Della. It's just her psychological stuff, you know. I suppose she

understands your new cousin thoroughly by now." The mother spoke with a touch of irony as if she were glad that *some* member of the family could understand Wynelle.

With the solemn tone of a martyr to the faith, Thelma nodded her head, and glancing toward Wynelle, muttered, "Yes. *Paramuthetic paranoidism.*"

Then her brother spoke up indignantly.

"I resent that!" he burst out.

The rest of the family had paid no attention to Thelma's long words, but he insisted: "Dad, she's telling our guest that she's making up all that about the airplane to console herself for some unpleasant thing that has happened. I know because that's one of her stock phrases she uses when she wants to take somebody down. You know yourself she doesn't know beans about psychology. She's just hunted up words in the dictionary and she tries to sound smart! I think it's time that sort of hooey was stopped."

The deep red flamed up in Thelma's skinny neck and all the way up under her glasses. Hatred raged in her eyes as she glared at her brother. In offended dignity, trembling with anger, she rose from the table and stalked out of the room while her father broke out crossly, "What's all the row about, you two? Why can't we have one meal in peace? Alberta, I'm going now. No, I won't wait for dessert. We had to wait so long to start dinner, with half the family late, that I will have to pass up my dessert. That's what it is to be in my position!"

Out he stormed, leaving everyone to wonder what position required a man to refrain from desserts.

Wynelle had hoped to have a chance to ask her cousin Dick about her new property, but he had not referred to it and there had been so much tension at the table that it did not seem a good time to bring up the subject. She had hoped sincerely that the vague reports of her grandmother Williams' uncongeniality with these relatives might be groundless. Now she felt as if she would like to get away and never come back. It was hard to see that there was anything nice in any of these people. But perhaps she was only tired. Perhaps they did not mean to be heartless. Richard had stood up for her, and Della had been pleasant enough in her way.

As they all got up from the table Richard smiled and came over to her side.

"How about a date tonight?" he asked eagerly.

Wynelle's heart sank. She was dogtired and she did not feel up to going out socially. She had so hoped for a nice quiet time in their home getting acquainted.

As she hesitated the front door bell rang and Emory Ames was ushered in. Mona became twittery at once and all smiles. It was hard for Wynelle to realize that she was the same cross grumbling girl she had been in their room before dinner. So that was the way some girls fooled the man they intended to marry! Was that how Mona had behaved before her first marriage? And was it perhaps why that marriage had had an untimely end? Wynelle felt suddenly as unsophisticated as a child. Her natural tendency had always been toward utmost sincerity and now she felt as if she had been thrust into the presence of something unclean.

Emory Ames seemed considerably older than Mona. He had a dark mustache but his hair was sprinkled with gray, and there were shabby-looking pouches under his eyes. He carried a cigarette in a long holder. He was immaculately dressed, and he looked Wynelle up and down when they were introduced, with obvious disapproval of her simple garb.

"Hi, Ames," greeted Richard debonairly. "How about a double date tonight, yes?"

"Not on your life, brat!" retorted Mona, laughingly but with fierce decision. "We are having this evening to ourselves, naze paw, ami?" She glanced archly up at her escort who smiled down at her and produced flowers. She screamed with delight and rushed to her room to pin them on and see to her make-up.

Nothing daunted, Richard grabbed Wynelle's arm.

"Okay, pig," he hurled back at his sister. "We can enjoy ourselves, too, without you! We'll go to a show. There's a good one at the Bijou. Come on, gal. By the way!" He stopped her short. "What is your name? I've forgotten."

"Oh!" gasped Wynelle, a little abashed. "It's Wynelle."

"Wynelle!" echoed Mona stridently issuing from her room again. "Good heavens! It's as bad as mine! Well, I'm sure I hope you'll have a good time tonight, Wyn-nelle. Though I shall probably call you something easier to remember—like Jane." She giggled. "We weren't sure when your telegram came with your name signed whether it was Wyn-nelle or Wine-nelle."

"Well, it's Nellie for me," announced Richard taking her arm again possessively. "And I'm going to use it so often that you all will get used to it. Come on, Nellie!" He pulled at her but she drew back.

It was nice to be wanted but she was by no means ready to let herself in for a long evening with this young man.

"Please, not tonight, Richard," she begged. "I am so tired I'm afraid I couldn't keep awake. I really have had a rugged time the last two days and I'm worn out. Let me get some rest first."

Richard begged but Wynelle finally won and soon excused herself and went off to bed, after helping Della with the dishes, much to that young lady's amazement, for it was Della's turn tonight to do them and unless some hard bargain had been made in return for favors none of the others was ever willing to help. The maid was there only two days a week and she left as soon as dinner was prepared.

"You know, I really think you are nice, in spite of your being so different and funny," stated Della as she wrung out the dish cloth at last and hung it up.

"You do?" smiled Wynelle amusedly. Although she did feel herself unsophisticated in comparison to these cousins, in some ways she felt infinitely older. They were all like so many un-governed children. "Well, I'm glad. I didn't know I was different and funny, but that's not surprising, I guess." She laughed.

Della studied her again with a puzzled look.

"Now there you are again! If I had said that to most people they would have been hurt, although when I said it I didn't mean to be rude, I was just thinking aloud. You aren't hurt and I don't know why. You *are* funny, but you're nice. For instance, I don't know anybody who would have come in and helped me like this if they didn't have to, or didn't think they would get something out of it themselves. You didn't. You really seemed to enjoy doing the dishes with me. I don't get it."

Wynelle smiled again and warmth began to creep into her heart again. Perhaps these people were lovable, if only she would put herself out to love them. She put her arm around Della's waist and gave her a little squeeze.

"Well, you're my own cousin, aren't you, even if we are only 'seconds?' And anyway, I do like to help. I know it's no fun to do dishes, especially by yourself, for I've done oodles of them. It isn't so bad if there's somebody to talk to and joke with while you do them."

"But you couldn't care anything about me, you know. So why would you care whether it was fun for me or not?"

Wynelle thought a long moment.

"Well," she said gently, "I don't know that I know how to say it very well, but I guess I care because God cares for me! And I know what it is to be lonely and to hate what you're doing." Her cheeks were pink with the effort of putting her shy thoughts into a form that this poor loveless girl could understand. In fact, Wyn-elle herself had never actually thought out what she had said. But the very saying of it made her heart grow warmer and she felt drawn to the girl. Perhaps many people would seem more lovable if they were loved and cared for. What a life this family lived. Everyone for himself. Self-centered as the life in Uniontown had been, yet there had been a basic care one for the other among the mother and sister and herself at least, even though there wasn't much show of affection. Could it be that God had really sent her east here after all, because there was an even needier family than her own? That was comforting, for she had begun to think that her coming was all the result of her own wilful dissatisfaction with life in general in Uniontown.

She climbed into the not-too-clean double bed and crawled to the far side nearest the wall, so that Mona could get in easily when she came. She felt grateful that this hard day was at an end.

Tomorrow she would go out and see her house!

CHAPTER 7

But the next day when she mentioned the house at breakfast Dick seemed to have a sudden desire for her to be treated like an honored guest. He instructed his wife to take the family car and show Wynelle around.

"Show her everything in town!" he ordered in a cordial bluster. "She might like to go out to the cemetery, too," he suggested. "Lots of tourists do, it's so old. There are some really humorous epitaphs on some of those old stones there," he went on, "and some of them date from the Revolutionary days. Yes, you mustn't miss that. You'd better start right in and see everything, because you likely have your time all planned, and later perhaps you will be wanting to take in some places farther afield, Washington and so on. No telling when you'll get back this way again."

Wynelle said that would be nice, and would the ride take them past her house?

"Oh, of course, of course," he assured her. "No need to hurry about that, though. Plenty of time for business. Take what pleasure you can first. Ha! Ha!" He slapped his knee as he rose from the table talking on about the wonders of Maple Grove and its environs.

"I tell you, Alberta, why don't you ride around this morning and then meet me for lunch at the club. I may be able to get off and take you myself out to the cemetery. That would be a nice trip. Any of the rest of you like to go along?"

"Not I!" spurned Della. "Not on your life. I'm playing a tennis doubles match off today at the country club. I may see you there."

"Oh," offered her father, "do you want to have lunch with us?"

"Not unless you'll stake the whole four of us, and I know that's far from your Scotch mind, my dear parent. No, let Snaz Robertson feed us. He's lousy with dough, and he won't miss it. Go on, folks, have a nice time among the dead!"

Wynelle did not look forward to the prospect of a long day spent in the sole company of Cousin Alberta with the possibility of Cousin Dick thrown in, but she was relieved that she seemed to be more like a welcome guest today than last evening, and there was nothing to do but accept the apparent hospitality with as good grace as she could.

She knew that her one cotton dress would not do at a country club, so she suggested to Alberta that perhaps it would be best for her to shop an hour or so first. Wynelle thought that in that way she might hurry through her shopping and inquire of someone the way to the late Mrs. Williams' house, and get a little glimpse of it all by herself. She did long to see what it was like, at least from the outside. It surely could not be much for apparently it was not of interest to Cousin Dick.

Alberta welcomed with glee the shopping tour. They would drive the fifteen miles to Middle City, she decided, for there was so little choice in Maple Grove. Wynelle could get what she wanted there and they could be at the country club in plenty of time for lunch with Dick. Alberta obviously was relieved not to have to tour Maple Grove this morning. They could do that the next day, she said.

So off they started. There was considerable difference of opinion when it came to selecting clothes. Wynelle's tastes did not coincide with Alberta's and yet Alberta almost insisted on certain things which Wynelle thought too dressy. "Because," Alberta said, "you don't want to feel *dowdy* when you go out with *us,* my dear." Wynelle wondered frantically whether she was wrong and her cousin was right. But the things Alberta wanted her to buy were not only more expensive than she thought she should afford, but they were not what Wynelle could use later. At last they reached a compromise on a white shantung suit which Alberta said would "do" that day at the club, although she did think it very plain. Wynelle tucked a gay flowered handkerchief in its pocket and bought a pair of tan and white spectator pumps and a tan handbag. None of the things were expensive, but she gave a little inward shudder as she realized that there was almost nothing left now of her first hundred dollars. She probably had to get back home sometime, and live in the meanwhile. She had decided during the night that she simply could not and would not stay very much longer at the Snellers'. As soon as she could find another place and decently make her farewell she would do so.

Of course if she sold her house she would not need to feel so strapped financially. But she must see it first, to decide that. Also, she must get about Maple Grove considerably more and find out whether she wanted to stay or not. If all the people were like those she had seen so far, she would just as soon spend her life in Uniontown.

The day was no less dull than Wynelle had feared when she started out. For the most part Cousin Dick and his wife discussed affairs and people whom she did not know, pausing only occasionally to offer her a word of explanation. They had frequent spats which were most embarrassing to Wynelle, but which seemed to be taken by them as a matter of course. In between and underneath all the flow of words Wynelle kept going back to the thought of her flier friends, wondering how they were, wondering if she would ever see them again, and whether she had done wrong to go on with her own life without making sure that they were all right. But what else could she have done?

As the day wore on Wynelle grew more and more eager to drive past her own house, but every time that she brought up the subject again Dick would brush it aside saying, "Oh, time enough for that. Let's have a good time while we can. I declare, this is fine. I don't often get a day off like this."

When late in the afternoon they arrived home after seeing what seemed like everything in the country and more, Wynelle felt as if she were under guard. She had thought she could slip out a few minutes before supper and take a little walk but there was always some reason why she must stay right in the house.

"Oh! I *hoped* you would help me a little with supper tonight," cried Alberta tying a soiled apron over her silk dress. "Della is not back yet and Mona *still* has a headache. Thelma is worse than useless when it comes to cooking, although she is right good at doing the dishes. *Would* you mind?"

So Wynelle stayed and helped. It seemed that there was nothing much to do, just set the table and put on the salt and pepper and bread and butter. But of course she was a guest and it was only right that she help out when she was asked. She tried hard not to feel resentment at their treatment of her. It was not that she would not have helped gladly, even more than she did, in fact she could have got the whole supper much more easily and efficiently than Alberta. But it was exasperating the way they all seemed to expect to run her life for her and give her no love or cordiality in return.

Supper dragged itself to an end with bickerings again and Wynelle felt heartsick. She offered to do the dishes herself and her offer was accepted with alacrity. It was Mona's turn to do them and while she had been able to stow away a fair amount of dinner, she still pleaded a headache and her mother excused her.

Wynelle decided that she would slip out early the next morning and take a look around the town. Surely nobody would object to her having a walk before breakfast.

But Richard was up early, too. And he was delighted to offer her his company. He took her past the little business section, all of which she had seen the day before, and up the one street of rather pretentious houses. Then he started home again.

"Is my little house anywhere near here?" asked the girl. "I would so like to see it."

"Your house!" exclaimed Richard. "Oh! You mean Aunt Ag's

old dump. No, that's away over the far side of town from here."

"The town isn't too big, is it?" suggested Wynelle. "Couldn't we walk by there? It's not time yet for breakfast."

"Good heavens no! It's a long way. I have no desire to wear out my feet this early in the day. Come on, let's take in this one more block and go home. A friend of mine lives in the big house up at the corner there. Maybe I can wangle an invitation for you and me to go there some time while you are here. They give a lot of parties."

So they went back to the house. And at breakfast Alberta announced that she had been asked to serve at the cake stall for her church's bazaar that afternoon, and they wanted her to bring two hundred cup cakes, as the woman who was to have contributed them had been called out of town. Would Wynelle be willing to help her this morning with the cakes and then help at the counter? There was always such commotion at those bazaars that Alberta never could get the change counted rapidly enough!

With a sinking heart Wynelle graciously agreed to help, but she made up her mind that by another day she, too, would have plans already made.

"This afternoon will be a *splendid* opportunity to introduce you to my friends," said Alberta squinting through her bifocals at the marks on her measuring cup. "I have been doing a *great* deal of entertaining lately, and I'm *all* worn out, and it will save me having to have people in, you know. This bazaar is always rather a social event as well as an opportunity to make money for the church. I really count it an *honor* to be asked to bake for it, because the woman who generally makes the cup cakes is simply marvelous when it comes to cakes. Everybody *raves* about hers. I'm so afraid that my poor little cakes won't even *compare* with hers!" She gave a little deprecatory laugh which said plainly, "I know very well that I can bake as well as any woman in the church." And she rattled on until Wynelle longed for quiet and peace.

During the afternoon Wynelle had opportunity to discover what Alberta had meant by the bazaar being a social event, for Alberta spent practically all of the time chatting with one or another. Sometimes if a friend stopped at her booth she would introduce Wynelle, but more often she would go shooting off across the room to seize upon some newcomer with "a very important message." Wynelle had the change to make and the wrapping and selling to do as well, and by dinner time she was worn out, unaccustomed as she was to standing continually.

She was called upon for help again with dinner, and what could she do but comply, since she was staying there in the home? But it looked as if she would soon become the family drudge if she stayed long enough. She simply must get out of here soon. But she couldn't leave the town without accomplishing the thing that had brought her east. Tomorrow without fail she made up her mind to see that house of hers!

Each morning at the breakfast table she had brought up the subject, and it was hastily brushed aside. She had mentioned it rather timidly at first, thinking that she must be careful not to upset any of the family plans in favor of her own interests. But nobody seemed to mind upsetting hers, and while she had no desire to retaliate, she felt that it was time for her to take her own life in hand and live it.

But her Cousin Dick had other plans. As he and Alberta were preparing for bed, he pulled at his tie impatiently while he said in a low voice, "If we can stall off that girl another couple of days, I think I have the house sold. Then I'll just have her sign the papers in a hurry, saying that the people are starting off for Europe or somewhere, and the deed will be done. I can easily prove to her that it's a wise move. I really think it is. The people who are looking at it are quite wealthy, and they plan to pay cash for it. That will ease our own situation quite a bit, my dear!" He gave a jovial slap to Alberta's nylon-clad back.

An unexpected circumstance had turned up at the bazaar which Wynelle decided to use.

"I met the aunt of a school friend of mine yesterday," she told them brightly the next morning. "The girl's grandmother lives here in town and would like to have me visit her. So I promised to go over there this morning. I have the address and it's not too far from here for me to walk. Nobody need take me." She spoke with firmness.

A worried frown appeared on Alberta's brow, for Dick had already gone to the office. Wynelle had timed her remark carefully.

"Oh, my *dear!*" cried Alberta with concern. "I couldn't *think* of letting you go way off there all *alone*. It's a long, long way. Couldn't you wait until a day when I have the car and could take you?"

"No. I promised I'd go today. The old lady is expecting me. And I really don't mind walking. At home I take long walks for pleasure. I shall enjoy it!"

"But you don't realize how *far* it is, I'm sure!" Alberta was quite frantic now. "I'm going to call Dick and see if he couldn't let me have the car today." She started for the telephone, but Wynelle walked out the front door while she was dialing the number, and called back to her,

"I would prefer that you didn't do that, Alberta, I am going to start right now, so I shall have plenty of time. Don't wait lunch for me, I gathered from what the aunt said that they would like me to stay. Good-by."

She started swiftly down the street, although she could hear Alberta calling to her to come back, that Dick said he would take her. She was determined to get off on her own a little while and find out for herself what sort of place her grandmother had left her.

She had a feeling that her cousin Dick might even take the

car and come in search of her, they had been so insistent upon escorting her everywhere. Of course it was nice of them to be solicitous for her but she would prefer that they show their concern by not making her help so much at housework and cake sales that she was kept from walking out by herself. They seemed a little inconsistent. However, they must be kind at heart and they probably meant well.

The day was bright and she did enjoy walking. She knew that she was starting out at an hour far too early for visiting the grandmother of her friend. She had planned to go straight to her own house and look it over before she went on to make her call.

Wynelle had thought to look up her grandmother's name in the telephone book and she knew the address, so rather than ask the Snellers for directions she thought she would walk a few blocks until she met someone of whom she could ask the way.

She turned down a pleasant street where some boys were playing ball. She thought that if anyone would know the streets of the town, boys would. Sure enough, they gave her detailed instructions. She left them and started off gaily, turning a corner behind a tall hedge just as Dick Sneller, cruising the streets looking for her in response to Alberta's telephone call, turned in the opposite direction. Fuming, he went up one street and down another, until at last he decided to go back to the office and wait until Wynelle would have reached the house of her friend. He would then call there and tell her he would stop for her and bring her home. That would look like a friendly gesture, and would guard against her going anywhere that he did not care to have her go.

But Wynelle was already on her way out to the edge of town, humming a gay tune as she went, and liking the look of things better and better as she went along.

"It's the last house on the left out Summit Street," the boys had told her, "kind of off from the rest. The road ends there. It's brown, with a lot of trees and bushes. It's real old, you know."

It was a good two miles that she had to walk and she began to be troubled about getting back in time to make her visit, when at last she came in sight of the end of the paved road.

Almost afraid to look to the left lest she be horribly disappointed, she stopped breathless. The houses had not noticeably deteriorated out this way; they were all pleasant places, in good repair, with pretty, well-kept lawns. But the boys had said her house was off from the rest. It might not be like them. She had tried all the way to imagine what she would find. She had so thoroughly made up her mind before she left Uniontown that her house was nothing of worth, that she was ready to expect little more than a shack. Now her eyes followed a smooth green lawn that sloped up a little, with a tiny stream glinting down at its right. And there at the top of the slope was her house!

Her heart stood still with delight.

It was small but it was a gem. Built of old, old stone, mossy with age, roofed with thick brown shingles that looked as if they had been cut by hand, it nestled among its greenery as if it had long ago found its heart's rest. A delicate pink rose vine rambled here and there across the walls. Lovely old steppingstones, worn smooth by the feet of many callers, marked the path to the front door. All was in perfect order and the scene breathed peace.

"Oh-h-h!" exclaimed Wynelle, clasping her hands in an ecstasy of appreciation at the very loveliness of the place, and trying to take in the fact that this precious home was really hers.

Forgetting that someone might be living there, she sped up the walk with the feeling that she would like to take the dear little house into her arms and hug it to her. It seemed to have such a welcome loving personality. Oh, what a joy to find a place like this to come to, after the cold comfort of the Sneller household! She would move right over here and make it her home. She knew without further thought that this would be home to her now as long as she lived.

She was about to put her hand on the polished old brass handle, just to try it, when all of a sudden it opened and a young man started out the door.

He stopped short and stared at Wynelle and rubbed his eyes. And Wynelle stared back at him.

CHAPTER 8

"You are alive!" he said with deep solemn joy. "I've searched and searched for you."

A glad light came into Wynelle's face that was beautiful to see.

"And I searched for you, too," she said shyly. "I was afraid you had been killed!" Two big tears of relief suddenly welled over and slid down her cheeks.

All at once the young man put out both his lean strong hands and grasped her arms gently. It was like the comforting hold he had taken in the plane and Wynelle looked trustingly up into his face.

"I'm *glad* you have come!" he told her. "But how did you find me?"

"Find *you*? I wasn't even looking for you just now. I came to see my house! What I want to know is how *you* came to be here?"

For a puzzled moment Roger Blackstone gazed at Wynelle and then he said, "Come in a minute and let's talk this over."

He put her in Grandmother Williams' rocker and he took the chair opposite. There was a little table beside it and he reached over to its small shelf and pulled out a photograph album. While he leafed through it a moment Wynelle glanced about her.

The morning light was dancing through leaded casement panes on the old wide-pegged boards of the oak floor. There were braided rugs of warm colors here and there which she supposed Grandmother Williams had made herself. Shelves each side of the big stone fireplace held books from floor to ceiling. Amber-colored net curtains caught the sunshine and emphasized it in a thousand sparkles in two fine old glass candlesticks on a drop-leaf table.

Across a tiny hallway Wynelle could see that there were two
bedrooms, simply furnished, mostly in antiques. There was a
large kitchen behind the fireplace, but she could only glimpse
a corner which showed bright yellow curtains.

Wynelle smiled. This was home! It had been a real home for
a long, long time. Its beams were seasoned with heartaches and
joys and its very walls breathed peace.

Then she noticed that the young man had looked up from his
book and was studying her. He glanced down once more and
then up at her again. His gaze was not rude or disrespectful, only
full of wonder.

"Could you by any chance be this little girl?" he asked gently.
He stood up and brought her the book, kneeling beside her to
point out the picture. Wynelle glanced at the snapshot. It was
one her mother had taken of her when she graduated from gram-
mar school several years before.

"Why, yes!" she cried in amazement. "Where did you get it?
My mother must have sent one to my grandmother. Is that why
it's here? But I still don't know why *you* are here. Are you the
real-estate agent?"

Roger laughed then, a hearty laugh like a boy.

"No, I'm not. Do you need one? Say, you're not going to *sell*
this place are you?" He seemed concerned.

"Indeed no!" said Wynelle. "I'm in love with it. I had no idea
it was so charming. I thought it would be some little old shack
that was half tumbled down! I can't get over it."

Roger sobered down.

"You didn't think that after all that Gram Williams did for me
I would let her beloved home go to wrack and ruin, did you?
Remember this has been my home for the last fifteen years, and
I—" his voice lowered and he almost choked on the words, "I love
it, too."

"Oh-h!" breathed Wynelle with a kind of shock in her tone.
"You must be—you must be that boy—that—"

A shadow came across Roger's face and he stood up tall and lean and sorrowful. He looked her steadily in the eyes as if to gauge her attitude toward him as he said slowly, "Yes, I'm 'that' boy, Roger Blackstone. If you have come," he spoke rather frigidly now, "to take over the place, I assure you that I shall make no trouble. Of course I was in the hospital a couple of days after the accident, so that things are not just as I would like to turn them over to you, but after a few hours' work I can have everything shipshape and be out of here, out of your way. I have not intended to stay! I have lived here since Mrs. Williams' death only to care for the property."

His voice had grown steadily colder and his manner stiffer, as if he had withdrawn little by little into his shell.

Wynelle still sat staring at him trying to fit together the pieces of the story as they had always been represented to her, and they did not fit. She was watching his fine sensitive mouth and his firm chin as he talked, and the way he held his head. She was remembering again the respectful, almost reverent way he had guarded and cared for her, a total stranger. Her mother had always spoken of the child that her mother-in-law had taken as if he were worthless, the no-account offspring of a criminal. This man was wonderful, a prince of a man. She could not reconcile the two.

Then all of a sudden as she remained silent she became aware of the hurt in his eyes and she sprang up, taking in all that he had been saying.

"Oh, please!" she begged, "don't think that I feel that way about you. I was just trying to understand everything. I haven't come to put you out, and I wouldn't now if I had! Why!" She drew nearer and put her hand on his sleeve. "*You*—saved my life, have you forgotten?"

"Oh, that!" he said brusquely. "That was nothing."

"Nothing!" she cried. "It was *everything* to me. And more than just saving my life, it was the way you did it. You were so—so gentle, and thoughtful, and kind, and you risked your own life to save me. I figured it all out afterwards what you must have done, how you waited to pull your own rip cord until you were free of mine. Oh, I've gone over and over the whole thing, and I've been *so* troubled about you! I have gone to sleep every night praying for you, and I will never forget how comforting it was to have you hold me that way!"

Wynelle's earnestness was shining in her eyes now and her cheeks were very pink as she tried to make him see how grateful she was.

Gradually the hard, hurt look melted from his face and he smiled a slow smile. It transformed his lean face until Wynelle thought that must be what an angel looked like, if angels smiled.

"You're making a whole lot of a small thing," he said humbly. "There wasn't anything else to do. We didn't know what minute the plane would explode."

"Really?" exclaimed Wynelle, aghast. "Well, it *wasn't* a small thing, and nobody will ever persuade me that it was. And most men I know wouldn't have done it just the way you did, and I thank you; more than you will ever know, I thank you."

Roger continued to look down at her, gazing deep into her eyes. Then he swallowed hard.

"I appreciate those words. More, I guess, than *you* will ever know," he said in a low voice.

There was deep meaning in his tone, as if there was a background of suffering behind it. Wynelle had a sudden unreasoning desire to take this young man into her arms, as if he were a little boy, and rock him there in her grandmother's chair. It was absurd for her to feel such sympathy for an utter stranger. And yet he was not a stranger at all. He had saved her life! And not only that, but he was in a way a member of the family, since he had been brought up by her own grandmother. She had a feeling that she had known him all her life.

She smiled warmly.

"You don't know," she told him, "how good it feels to think that I have a real friend here in town. I am staying with people I don't know well, and so far we don't seem to have much in common."

"I'm glad if you will count me a friend," he said earnestly. "I wish you would feel free to call upon me in that capacity for anything at any time. It would give me great pleasure."

Wynelle had a swift mental glimpse of the boys she had known at home in Uniontown, as if they were ranged in a row beside this one. Harry Harper, and the greasy Bud Hendricks, and Lambert Odum. No wonder she had not been satisfied with them when there was in the world a young man like this. She could not imagine any one of those boys inspiring in her the confidence and trust that she had in this man, although she had known him scarcely more than an hour or so in all, and those boys she had known all her life. This was the sort of man who would never think of himself first. He was a gentleman through and through, the type of gentleman that seemed to be fast passing out of existence. His courtesy was not so much in his good manners as in his whole attitude to her and her situation. Something glad and strong welled up in her to think that there was such a man and that she had even a slight acquaintance with him.

Wynelle was not aware of the joyous light in her face, and she did not understand why she felt so much drawn to this stranger. But all of a sudden she looked at her watch, realizing that the morning must be wearing away and she had a call to make. She had better be getting on before she made a fool of herself. She was so relieved to find him alive and well that she must be emotionally unbalanced.

He still stood watching her respectfully, as if awaiting her wish as to what he should do about the house. But she had forgotten even her beloved house for the moment. She wanted to make sure that Roger Blackstone really was unhurt, and that all was well with him.

"Did you have a terrible fall?" she asked. "You were in the hospital, weren't you?" She looked up at him with concern in her face, and did not know how lovely she looked to him, nor how sweet to his heart was the fact that she cared.

"A little concussion," he said carelessly. "That was all. We were very fortunate."

"Any concussion is serious, I know that much," answered Wynelle. "But how about your friend. Was he hurt?"

"Yes, pretty badly, although not too seriously. He tried to make a landing but there was no clear strip and he was pretty well shaken up. One leg is broken and there was a slight fracture of the skull, but the doctors assure me he will be all right in time. I'm going up to Washington again tomorrow to see him. It was only by a miracle that all of us weren't blown to bits or burned to death. The Lord was good to us."

He spoke seriously, not flippantly as so many of the young people of Wynelle's acquaintance did when they mentioned the name of the Lord. She noticed it and wondered. After a long moment of studying him she said,

"You're different from most fellows, do you know it?"

The shadow came across his face again, but he smiled a little as he said,

"I've been told so before. Not always so kindly."

Wynelle caught her breath in remorse.

"Oh, I didn't mean to say anything to hurt you," she assured him. "I meant that I think you are—*wonderfully* different." She paused, a little embarrassed.

His look softened and he gazed almost yearningly at her as she sat with her eyes down now, a lock of her soft brown hair falling over her forehead. She seemed quite unconscious of herself as she turned her eyes up once more to his with tender sympathy.

"You're rather different yourself, you know," he said reverently in a low tone. "I have never known any girls very well," he admitted with a little chuckle, "but the ones I have known seemed to me rather empty-headed and self-centered, and I hope I'm not too critical. Most of them would have screamed and fainted or made some sort of a scene up there in the plane and made it difficult to help them. You were a brick."

She grew pink under his honest gaze and his compliment.

"I should think that the least I could have done was to keep quiet and do as you told me," she said modestly. "After all, I couldn't have helped myself."

"But that's just where you're different from most girls," he said. "They all think they know how to run themselves and everybody else." He grinned. "I guess I'm too particular." Then changing the subject, he went on, "But when do you want to get in here? I can be out in a very short time."

"Oh!" she cried with a sort of sudden shock as she realized that she was in the position of putting him out of his beloved home. She found herself trying to think of some way to arrange things so that he could stay. She avoided the issue a moment so as to give herself time to think. "What are you doing now? I mean, do you work here in town, or . . ." She left the sentence hanging in mid-air for him to take up and finish.

"Not exactly," he said. "I have very little business here in town, even though it is the county seat. I've never been popular here, you know." Wynelle noticed the shadow again. It was very deep this time, but there was no bitterness in his tone. "I have hung out my shingle in Middle City. It's a fair-sized city about fifteen miles away. Perhaps you've heard of it."

"Oh, yes," replied Wynelle. "I was there yesterday doing some shopping. I had no clothes, of course, when I got here." She laughed.

"Oh!" he cried. "I forgot about your suitcases. I have them in my car. The plane was burned pretty badly, but they are not hurt, I think. I brought them home with me, for I was determined I'd find you. I only got here a few minutes before you did. I've been combing the countryside ever since they let me out of the hospital.

I was just starting back to search further when you arrived. Boy! Am I glad you're all right." He smiled at her in genuine relief.

There was sweet comradeship in knowing that each cared that the other was safe, and Wynelle felt strangely happy, happier than she had ever been in all her life. She did not analyze her feeling at the moment. It was just a gladness. And she found herself loth to leave and go to make her call.

"It will be a great help to me to have my things," she cried. "I couldn't afford to replace them all, and I've been getting along on very little. Thank you so much!" She stood up. "I guess I ought to go now," she said hesitatingly. "I have promised to see someone this morning out on State Street, and I'm afraid I'm going to be quite late." She gave a merry laugh as if she really didn't care whether she was late or not, for she was enjoying every minute of their time together.

Roger offered to drive her to State Street, and then he brought up the subject of the house again.

"Can I be of service in helping you to move in here?" he asked.

"Move in? Oh no!" she said. "There is no hurry about that at all. In fact, I'd like to talk it over with you, what's best to do with it, you know." She had suddenly realized as she talked that it would not do to suggest that he simply stay on here, for she sensed that he would never consent to keep her out of her own house unless he was convinced that it would be advantageous to her in some way.

He looked about the pleasant living room, almost as if he were saying farewell to it, she thought, and then he said, "You ought to get a good price for it, if you really want to sell it. I don't suppose you would be interested in keeping it unless you were going to stay on here to live, although it should make a very nice income property for you, if you care to rent it. What did you have in mind?"

They had started out the door now and were walking slowly

around the house to the garage. Wynelle had to stop and exclaim over every bush and ask about it. The garage took her fancy, too. It was not old like the house, of course, but it was built along the same architectural lines, and vines like those on the house were beginning to cover it so that it fitted snugly into the scene as if it had always been there. Everything was so trim and beautifully kept that Wynelle was delighted.

"Oh, I just *couldn't* rent this," she cried. "I don't suppose that I'd ever find any tenant who would keep it the way you have!" she exclaimed, suddenly realizing that only love for a place would have made people want to keep it looking so charming. "Besides," she added, "I've seriously considered staying here in Maple Grove."

The young man's face brightened.

"It's a nice little town, I guess," he said sadly. "I still like it although it has never showed its friendly face to me. Still, I don't blame people for that. I would have felt the same way toward some other kid, I suppose, if I hadn't been through the mill first. And I can honestly say I'm glad for all the hurts. I've learned a lot more than I would have if everything had gone my way." He smiled gently, the smile that seemed to Wynelle to come from within him somewhere.

"I told you you were wonderfully different," she said again shyly. "Perhaps you will tell me about all that some day." She spoke very gently. "I don't think I know much about real trouble," she went on wistfully. "I've never been very happy, but then I've never had things so very hard either. I'm just a sort of in-between person, neither very wise nor very foolish, neither very good nor very bad."

He chuckled.

"Most people would give a lot to be as temperate as that," he laughed. "But you did tell me in the plane that you are a Christian," he said as if wanting to reassure himself.

"Well, yes," assented Wynelle, "but I don't think I'm even a very good Christian. I try to do right, and I've always gone to Sunday

School and church and all that. I've even taught a Sunday School class. But I don't think I've anything to brag about. In fact, none of religion seems as real to me as I could wish it did."

Roger was silent a long moment while they both looked off across the field to the heaps of puffy white clouds on the skyline.

"It can't, apart from the Cross, you know." He said it as if from deep experience and Wynelle found herself longing to know what he meant. There was depth of understanding, and sympathy, and potential comfort in him of a sort she had never known. Yet from all she had heard of him, and from what he had said himself, it would seem that his life had never been free from sadness.

He helped her courteously into his coupe, not a new model, but clean and shining.

As he climbed in beneath the wheel she was conscious of a feeling of cosiness and safety. It felt good to be shut in there with this man. He was one to be trusted thoroughly.

"I don't quite understand what you mean by that about the Cross," she said in a puzzled tone. "I guess I'm pretty ignorant about religion."

"Probably no more so than most of us," he assured her. "I wouldn't have understood anything about it or ever heard of it, I guess, if gram—I mean your Grandmother Williams—hadn't sent me to a real honest-to-goodness Christian college, where I had a professor who knew the Lord and lived close to Him. It was he who taught me how to let the Cross become a practical thing in my life. I was a pretty tough kid, and I guess I made gram plenty of trouble. But when I really got to know the Lord, that changed all the hard things of life so that they didn't hurt any more, and all the bitterness I had felt for the people here in Maple Grove disappeared."

There was a glad triumphant ring to his voice while he said this that made Wynelle wonder. She had never heard anybody, not even her minister, talk like this. Who ever heard of being actually glad for sorrow and trials? She stole a glance at the man beside her. It was hard to believe that he was real.

He turned a blazing smile upon her that seemed like the light of heaven itself. But she gave a little shiver, for she felt as if she were a very small worm somewhere far outside of such glory, and that the smile could not be meant for such as she.

"Are you chilly?" he asked instantly. "It's right cool this morning. I'll close this window if you like."

His solicitude touched her.

"Oh my no," she replied. "I like the breeze. I wasn't cold, I was just—well, I guess I was just sort of scared."

"Scared?" he asked puzzled. "Of what? Me?" He grinned boyishly.

But she was serious now.

"No, but what you said seemed to put you so very far above me. It sort of made me dizzy!"

He laughed, in a comradely way.

"If you only knew how low and small I feel most of the time," he said, "you wouldn't worry about that. But I think I know what you mean. May I come and take you for a ride some time and tell you more about it?"

"Oh, I would love that!" cried Wynelle.

"Tomorrow evening?" he asked.

"Yes, that will be fine."

They drew up at the house on State Street.

"Is this where you live?" he asked. "Shall I come for you here?"

"Oh no, I'm at 811 Main Street, at Snellers'. Mrs. Sneller is my second cousin, you know."

"Oh-h!" responded Roger slowly as if taken aback. "Oh, of course." He gave a wry smile. "I guess they won't be very glad to see me, but I'll come."

"Even if they won't, I will!" said Wynelle with a gay smile. But afterward she remembered his look when she had told him she was living at Snellers', and she wondered at it.

CHAPTER 9

AT THE TABLE that night Cousin Dick was all cordiality.

"I hear you found some friends here in town," he said pleasantly. "The Watsons are nice people, some of the best in town. Good solid, respectable people, who pay their debts. I've always heard that they have a fair-sized sockful stowed away for a rainy day. I like to see people who respect the good old American dollar. I don't like to see them squeeze it until it squawks, you understand," he chuckled, "but they say money talks and by George I like to hear it!" He slapped his knee at his own joke. His family did not rally with a laugh for they had heard his pun so many times that it did not seem funny to them.

"By the way," he went on genially to Wynelle, "I have good news for you. I think you are in a fair way to make a nice little sum yourself. We have your house sold for you. At a very good price, too. The buyers are anxious to get in immediately, so I arranged for you and me to go down to my office the first thing in the morning and sign the papers. They are going to pay all cash if they can have it right away. That's the nicest, easiest way to settle things, no strings to it, just take the money, sign the deed, and it's done." He smiled broadly.

Wynelle gasped.

"Oh!" she cried. "Why, I don't want to—that is, I don't know yet what I'm going to do with my house."

Dick laughed nervously.

"Don't you worry about that," he assured her. "That's what lawyers are for, to advise people who don't know what to do. This is a good sale, and the best price you are likely to get. The house is growing older all the time, and of course that means deterioration. The quicker we can get it off your hands, the better for you. It's never wise to try to hold property if you get a good price for it. Besides you are a young girl alone, and living away out west it wouldn't be easy for you to try to manage it. There's no end of red tape and fuss to renting, and it's always hard on a house. People don't take care of what's not their own. Best thing is to sell. If you get your price, that is, and we have. These people are paying ten for it, a good thousand more than I thought we could get. Of course we have some little repairs to do, and that will come out of the price, but you will have a nice little nest egg, my dear. Nearly ten thousand good American dollars is a sum not to be sneezed at, eh?"

He went rattling on about real-estate values, and Wynelle listened aghast. Ten thousand dollars did sound like a wonderful sum to her. There were many things she could do with that much, things she had always longed to do. She could take some trips and see something of the world, and she could even go to college if she chose to. She had always wanted to have more schooling than the two years of business training she had taken in Uniontown. Was her cousin right, perhaps, in urging her to sell?

But when she pictured to herself the little brown house snuggled there among its greenery, the lovely sloping lawns, the pleasant living room where she had had such a delightful visit with that wonderful young man this morning, and when she remembered his wistful look as he said, "You're not going to *sell* this place, are you?" her heart cried out against it. She scarcely knew what to say to Dick, or how to answer him. He was still talking and evidently did not expect an answer. He was simply taking for granted that she would follow his advice, as of course he knew more than she did about values, and the wisdom of owning or renting property.

She had not mentioned the fact that she had seen the house. She was not trying to hide it, but she had a strange feeling that

Dick would not be pleased at her acting on her own initiative.

She was still trying to think of some way to tell him politely and gracefully that she had seen the house and was not ready to make up her mind to sell it yet, when he pushed back his chair and said,

"Well, I'll take you down to the office with me the first thing in the morning. You be ready at eight. I don't like to keep clients waiting. There won't be a thing for you to do but sign your name. I've tried to arrange everything so that it will be perfectly simple for you."

Wynelle stood up and shook her head.

"But I'm not at all sure yet that I want to sell the house," she said with quiet determination. She did not see the worried frown on Alberta's bulging forehead, nor the wicked glee in Della's face as she caught the cloud of discomfiture on her father's red puffy face. "I have quite fallen in love with the place, and I have been thinking perhaps I would like to live here, if I can get a good job."

Dropping his high-handed manner in an instant, and casting a warning glance at Alberta, Dick spoke placatingly.

"Well, well, well!" he exclaimed. "We are glad that you like our little town so much. I don't blame you. I doubt if you will find as nice a town anywhere. It's respectable and quiet and all of the people here are well-to-do. Just a good old American village, you know, ha! ha!"

He took a step over toward Wynelle and smilingly seemed to take possession of her and draw her almost against her will to the living room, where he sat down opposite her and went on talking, although Wynelle had been sure before he rose from the table that he had been on his way out to an appointment.

"If you really want to stay," he said, "I think I can fix you up with a job. It is good to find a young girl who is intelligent enough to want to handle her own affairs. And I will be glad to take the time to go over everything connected with the house with you, my dear. Of course you must do as you please in this matter.

We wouldn't want to force you to go against your own wishes, but my colleagues and I have all agreed that the very best thing you could do with the property is to unload it. We have had a good deal of experience, you must remember. We have found that especially women alone are much better off if their money is in good dependable stocks or government bonds, than in real estate. The depreciation is so great in these changing times that one never knows when the bottom will drop out of things and there you are left with a house on your hands that nobody wants. It would cost quite a bit, you know, for you to keep up a whole house, just for yourself. And it would hardly be respectable for you, a young girl, to live there alone. You have to think of that in a small town like this. And believe me, you don't want tenants these days. The people who would pay the small rent that your house would bring would not be likely to be the type who would care for the place. You see, when you look at the proposition from all sides, there is only one answer, to sell. And now that these people have offered such a good price, I really would advise you to take it. No telling when there will be such an opportunity again."

He talked so fast and all that he said sounded so plausible that Wynelle felt as if she were caught in a whirlwind. He was such a practical-minded man that she could not bring herself to tell him that she didn't care about the money, that she had seen the house and had fallen in love with it; that it was like home to her, and she never wanted to part with it. It seemed like the only real home she had known since she was a little girl and her father had died. This little brown house seemed to stretch out its arms to her with such a cheery loving welcome! And she kept seeing the winning smile of the young man she had found there; she scarcely knew whether it was the house or his personality that drew her so strongly. But all this she could not tell to her cousin Dick!

So all that she answered was, "We- e-ell," hesitatingly.

And immediately he snatched that up and said in a relieved tone, "That's right, my dear. I knew you were intelligent above the average. Some women are so foolish about business affairs, and it's hard to make them see good sound common sense. Always ruled by their whims, they are. Believe me, I know! You can't be a lawyer in a small town for twenty-five years without getting to know a thing or two about women! Ha! Ha!"

He rose and started for his hat, calling something to Alberta about when he expected to be home.

But Wynelle was troubled. She had a feeling that her little brown house was about to be snatched from her unceremoniously, and she felt guilty about her sudden love for it. Perhaps Dick was right, and she was foolish. What if she held the house and couldn't afford to keep it up? It would need repairs from time to time of course. All houses did. They would be expensive. She had heard property owners discuss their bills many a time. They always said that they never were free from expenses of one kind or another. If the house were allowed to deteriorate then she never would be able to sell it, at least not at a good price. If only she could get away by herself and think the thing out. She disliked being rushed into the whole matter this way. How she would like to have a talk again with Roger Blackstone. He had promised to come and take her for a ride, but that was not until tomorrow evening. This must be decided, according to Dick, before tomorrow morning.

As she sat mulling it all over there on the couch where Dick had left her, Richard Jr., breezed into the room.

"Hi, Nellie," he greeted her. "How about that date we were to have? I can't let a pretty cousin go to seed like this. There's still a good show on at the Bijou. I've seen it but I don't mind going again. I won't have to watch the show this time, I can cast my eye around for the pretty girls, ha! ha!" He often ended his sentences with the same self-gratifying mirth that his father did.

Wynelle flinched under it. His remarks were not actually vulgar, but he reminded her somewhat of Harry Harper. She had to make an effort to be pleasant.

"Go ahead and get a pretty girl, Richard!" She forced a teasing smile. "I have letters to write home tonight."

"Aw, I didn't mean *you* weren't pretty, Nellie," he grinned. "Matter of fact, I think you are. There's something sort of different about you, you know." He sat down close to her on the couch. "Sometimes when I get to looking at you I can really get steamed up over you, believe it or not. I admit you don't look as smart as some girls, but there's something nice and soft and sweet about you that I really like." He grabbed one of her hands and squeezed it, patting her bare arm with his other hand.

Wynelle shrank from his touch and sprang up.

"No, really?" she said mockingly with an attempt at a gay laugh although she did not feel so gay as disgusted. "Well, I am afraid I'll have to deprive you of my pleasant company tonight. I'm going to get those letters off."

"Oh gosh! Nellie," he cried, "I didn't mean to hurt your feelings. I mean I really *do* like you."

"Nice of you, my friend," she threw back as she went toward the desk in the corner of the room. "Save your breath and get on to your show."

"No, I won't!" he insisted. "I'll wait until you finish your letters, doggone you, and then we'll walk down town and mail them. At least you'll stop at the drug store and have a sundae, won't you?"

Wynelle laughed again, although she smothered a sigh.

"Oh, sure, I guess so," she answered as if he were a child.

He hung around, annoying her with his vapid conversation while she wrote, until at last she gave it up after one letter to her mother, and they started down to the little business section.

They had just mailed her letter and were starting into the drug store when someone else arrived at the door at the same moment, a tall lean young man who stood aside to let Wynelle pass.

When she saw him she caught her breath.

"Why, hello!" he said lifting his hat to Wynelle.

"Hi!" she answered beaming with pleasure. Then she looked toward her cousin. "Richard, do you know Roger Blackstone? I feel that it's rather ridiculous for me to try to introduce two old residents of Maple Grove. You have probably known each other for years!"

Richard stared hard at Roger, and shrugged.

"Oh, I guess everybody knows *him,*" he said with an edge of contempt.

Roger had put out his hand so that Richard could scarcely avoid shaking it, but Richard was slow about returning the handshake and it was anything but hearty.

Even in the dim light Wynelle could see the deep red steal up in Roger's face, but there was no bitterness in his tone as he said to her pleasantly,

"It's a lovely evening, isn't it!"

"Yes," she answered eagerly. "We were mailing a letter and just came in for a sundae. Won't you join us?" She was aware of Richard's glowering looks, but she reasoned that she had not desired this little outing with Richard, he had insisted on it, and so she had a right to invite whom she pleased.

Roger hesitated, obviously about to refuse, but Wynelle looked up straight into his eyes and said seriously, "Please! I have been wishing I could see you. There are a couple of questions I would like to ask you."

So, quite as if Richard were not there looking sullen, Roger graciously seated Wynelle and took the seat opposite, leaving the vacant place beside her for Richard.

The atmosphere was somewhat strained at first, but Wynelle and Roger got to talking cordially in no time, even though Richard sat back disapprovingly and tried to act as if Roger were not there at all. He puffed on one cigarette after another, and leaned across Wynelle trying to speak right into her face and so cut Roger out of the conversation. But Wynelle cleverly brought Roger into it again and finally Richard arose gloomily and stalked over to the other side of the store to buy an evening paper.

Wynelle had wanted to bring up the subject of her house to ask Roger's advice, but she had suddenly realized that if she did it in front of Richard it would look as if she did not trust his father's wisdom. So now she took the opportunity to say softly,

"My cousin has a sale for my little house. Do you think I should let it go?"

Without a change of countenance, quite as if they were mentioning the weather, or the ball game next day, Roger asked,

"What do they offer?"

"Ten thousand. He says that's a good price, that I ought to snap at it."

A flicker of deep concern passed across Roger's face but Richard returned just then and he could say no more. Only with his eyes he showed her his disapproval and then said, "I should say not! The Yanks will certainly have to do a *lot* better than that to win."

Just for an instant Wynelle looked bewildered and then with a twinkle of dawning comprehension she answered calmly, "I guess maybe you're right. It's nice to have the word of an expert." And they went on discussing the World Series situation as if they had talked of nothing else.

Roger took care to reach for the checks when they came and paid for all three treats. Wynelle noted that Richard made little or no demur. Then Roger thanked them for their short time together and excused himself on the plea of work that must be done that night.

Wynelle stepped out into the darkness with a warm feeling of gladness that she had a friend who understood and upon whom she could depend. But Richard broke out with, "How on earth did you happen to come across that dimwit? He certainly hasn't wasted much time getting into your good graces, has he! That's just what we were all afraid he would do if you came east. Of course he would like to freeze onto that house of Aunt Ag's, and I suppose he thinks he can wheedle you into letting him have it somehow. But he will find out that he can't. My dad knows a thing or two about law that that fellow doesn't."

Wynelle could hardly believe her ears.

"Why on earth would you talk that way about Roger Blackstone?" she asked indignantly. "I think he seems like a fine young man. My grandmother always thought the world of him."

"Oh, *she* did, of course. But she was hipped. Old women sometimes do get that way, you know, silly over some young fellow. No, he really is no account. Didn't you know his father was a criminal, a *murderer*?"

"I remember long ago that grandmother said there was some tragedy in his life, but what would that have to do with Roger now? He has made good in his life, hasn't he? I understood he graduated from law school and set up practice."

"Oh, who told you that? He did, likely."

"Yes," admitted Wynelle stoutly, writhing inwardly over Richard's tone, "he told me himself."

"Well, that doesn't mean anything, of course." He spoke contemptuously. "I doubt if the fellow ever even finished college, let alone law school." Richard omitted to state that he himself had had difficulty getting through high school and had been thrown out of college in his first year. "You can't trust that guy," he went on. "We have always known that, we who have lived here in the same town with him all these years. Dad and mother tried their best to keep Aunt Ag from taking him, but she would do it. It sort of separated the family, her being so stubborn about it all. I just barely remember the whole thing but it wasn't very pleasant."

Wynelle was silent a few moments. Her heart wanted to stand up for the stranger who had befriended her so wonderfully, yet after all, she would have to admit that she really didn't know anything about him except what he himself had told her, and this young man was her cousin and the son of her host. She could not be actually rude to him.

"Well," she said at last, "I may not know many facts about Roger, but I do know that he was wonderful to me and acted like a perfect gentleman. In fact he risked his life for me." She spoke with gentle reverence as if she would never forget what Roger had done for her, no matter what else might be proved against him.

"Whaddaya mean, risked his life!" snorted Richard. "Where did you ever know him?"

Wynelle was so indignant at Richard's attitude that it was hard for her to speak calmly.

"He helped me when the plane caught fire," she said with heat. "He jumped with me and guarded me in every possible way."

"Oh-h-h!" Richard sneered now. "Is *that* the story! So *he* is your hero, is he? Ha! Ha! Ha!"

Wynelle was so furious now that she could not speak.

"I get it all now! He's the one, then, who put it into your head to come east and stir up a mess over the house. Nice guy! Well, that's just what I would expect of him."

"*That is not true!*" fumed Wynelle between set teeth. "I never saw him until he got on the plane at Cleveland. I didn't know who he was."

"O-ho!" roared Richard in derision. "So that's it! The plot thickens. You certainly fell for the guy in a hurry, didn't you!"

Wynelle stopped short and turned upon him.

"Richard Sneller," she stormed, "you are behaving perfectly detestably. I don't care to walk home with you now or at any time."

She started swiftly away, but Richard started after her, calling, "Oh say, can't you take a little kidding? All right, come on, I won't tease you any more, if you don't like it."

He hurried after her and snatched her arm. She jerked away but in doing so one foot slipped off the curbstone and twisted under her and she went down with a sickening pain in her ankle.

Richard tried to help her up and she struggled to rise but her foot gave way and she could not help crying out.

"Whatsa matter, Nellie?" asked Richard really concerned now. "D'ja get a bad bump? I'm sorry. I didn't mean to get you hurt, honest."

He seemed genuinely troubled, and Wynelle could only say, "Oh, that's all right. It was my own clumsiness."

But when he tried to pick her up, and could not, for he was not physically strong, she was secretly glad, for she shrank from his touch.

"Just let me alone," she said in a tense voice, "and I'll try to crawl home. It isn't far."

A car was passing and it slowed down at sight of them. The driver leaned out and called,

"Anybody hurt?"

Wynelle's heart leaped. She knew that voice. But before she could answer Roger had recognized her and was out of the car in an instant, stooping beside her.

"Are you hurt?" he asked in a low voice.

Wynelle felt such relief that she would like to have buried her head on his shoulder and sobbed. She managed a gay little laugh and said,

"Oh, I guess it's nothing much. I seem to have twisted my ankle, that's all." She tried again to rise, but Roger leaned over and lifted her easily, carrying her to the far side of the car and setting her down tenderly on the seat.

While Roger returned to get in on his own side, Richard stood hesitating, chagrined by the turn of events and the sudden appearance of the other young man. He had no desire to be taken home by the man he disliked but it angered him that Roger was paying no attention to him.

He stepped over to the car, although Roger had already started the motor, and leaning across Roger he said,

"Do you think you'd better have a doctor, Nellie?"

Wynelle shook her head and tried to make light of her pain.

"Oh, no, I guess not, thank you. It will probably be better in the morning if I rest it."

"Okay then," returned Richard. "Whatever you say. I'll be seein' you later."

He walked off airily down town again, whistling.

But on his way it occurred to him that it might bring down a good deal of criticism upon him at home if he did not even turn up to explain that the accident really was not his fault. So finding a friend who had a car down town, he persuaded him to drop him off at home. He did not see Roger's car outside, so he judged that he had deposited Wynelle and departed. But when he got inside he found that they had not arrived yet.

CHAPTER 10

Roger drove slowly for a block and then he stopped the car.

"You are shaking all over, aren't you?" he said sympathetically. "That's from shock. Your foot must be pretty bad. May I look at it?"

Trying hard to control her trembling, Wynelle nodded.

"I'm—just—be—ing—a b—baby, I guess," she said with tears in her voice.

"I think *not*," answered Roger with decision. "Any girl who could take her first parachute jump without batting an eye the way you did is no baby."

His fingers moved gently over her ankle.

"It's badly swollen already," he said, starting the car and turning swiftly down another street. "We'll get you to a doctor right away. Here," he reached back to the shelf behind him and produced a heavy sweater, "this is clean, if not beautiful. Put it on. You must keep warm."

Gratefully Wynelle slid into the sweater, several sizes too big for her, but soft and comforting. She hugged her arms about herself trying to quiet the shaking that possessed her.

In just a few moments they drew up in front of a doctor's house.

"This is a good guy," said Roger. "He's not as young as he once was, but he's had lots of experience with bones and sprains. He used to be our athletic coach when I was in high school."

Like a father carrying his little child Roger picked her up and took her to the door of the office.

"You'll have to ring the bell," he laughed. "I'm busy."

Wynelle gave a little comradely giggle and pushed the button.

It was wonderful having someone care for her like this. It was something she had never known since she was six and her father had died.

It was after hours but the doctor was busy and they had to sit quite a while in the waiting room. At last he saw them and his verdict was a bad sprain. Wynelle was to stay off her foot for three weeks. Her heart sank.

When Roger had her settled comfortably in the car again to take her home he noticed that she was silent and depressed.

"Not a pleasant prospect," he agreed. "I've had it to do myself a couple of times. It gets to be pretty boring. I think this doc knows his stuff, though. He says it won't be serious if you are careful."

"Oh, I don't mind that part," said Wynelle mournfully. "It's that I hate to be there at Snellers' like this. I had been wishing I could get away, but now I don't see how I can. I was going to get a job and find a room to live in somewhere. But how can I get a job now? And I can't afford to rent a room because this foot may take a lot of doctoring."

She sounded so forlorn and discouraged that Roger reached out his hand and laid it firmly and gently over her little cold one.

His touch was warm and consoling. It was not like a personal caress, that is, not like the way any of the boys she had ever known had tried to hold her hand. It was just a friendly, understanding comradeship, comforting and reassuring. She let her hand lie there in his and found herself taking a deep relieved breath, and her shaking subsided somewhat.

"You forget you have a home to go to if you want to," he reminded her.

"Oh!" she cried softly, "yes, so I do! Isn't that wonderful! But I realize that that wouldn't do right now. I don't suppose it would be exactly the thing to go and live there all alone anyway, and if I can't walk at all I certainly couldn't go now. I wouldn't any more ask one of my cousins to come there and help me than I would ask the president. No, it's nice to know I have the house, but that's out of the question right now. I guess I'm just chained to Snellers!" She sighed.

Roger was silent a few moments. Then he spoke in a serious tone.

"In that case, I'd try to find out why, if I were you."

Wynelle pondered that.

"What do you mean, 'why'? I suppose I'm being punished because I just would be silly and come running east here to see my house, when I should have been content to stay in that hole of a Uniontown that I've always hated."

Roger grinned sympathetically.

"I don't know about that," he said. "The way it looks to me, I think if you hadn't come you would have been out several thousand dollars."

Wynelle gasped.

"What do you mean?"

"Well, you say your cousin wants you to sell the place for ten thousand. That's absurd. It ought to bring thirteen at least. Houses are greatly in demand around here now, even as far from Washington as we are. I wouldn't go so far as to say that your cousin was trying to fleece you, but I'm quite sure that there must be a catch in it all somewhere."

"Really?" exclaimed Wynelle in horror. And then, in spite of her, Richard's remark about Roger wanting to get possession of the house came back to her. But that was ridiculous! How would his stopping her selling it too cheaply be of an advantage to him? It was wonderful that she had met him and that he had warned her in time, she assured herself. Yet try as she would she kept hearing Richard's words about Roger. She refused in her mind to believe them but they insisted upon returning. Oh, why hadn't she just stayed at home where she belonged, and not got into such a tangled lot of trouble? She sighed again and then she realized that Roger was talking to her.

"However," he said, "that's all beside the point. Sell your house if you like, of course. But it seems to me that the important thing for you is to find out why God has set you there at the Snellers' and is going to keep you there for at least three weeks in the most unpleasant position of being under obligation to them. There has to be a reason. Things like this don't happen accidentally, to a child of God."

"They don't?" said Wynelle wonderingly.

"Certainly not! If you had a dear child would you just let her go her own way and pay so little attention to her that she got herself into trouble? Do you think a loving God cares less about His children?"

"Well, no, I suppose not," said Wynelle slowly. "I just never thought He had time, I guess," she gave a shy little giggle, "to pay much attention to somebody so unimportant as me. I've never done anything for Him, to speak of."

"If you had, it wouldn't make any difference. It's *grace* He loves to show us, and that's *un*deserved kindness. Did you ever realize it's always *sinners* whom He saves? Jesus said He came not to call the righteous, that is, the people who could offer Him good works in return—or thought they could—but He came to call sinners, those who didn't deserve it at all!"

"Why, that's wonderful!" cried Wynelle in awe. "I never heard it put that way before." Tears came into her eyes. "Then that must be why He saved me, for I certainly am not worth much!"

Roger smiled gently. "Who of us is," he said, "until God gets hold of us and makes us something according to His mind? He has to work with each of us after we are saved. It's true that He has given us His righteousness as a gift, but He wants to work it out in our lives. That's why we have to have trials and that sort of thing. That's what I meant this afternoon by saying that what you believe never seems real apart from the Cross. It's only when we begin to let the Cross put the 'I' in us to death that the loveliness of the Lord Jesus Christ can be seen."

Wynelle hardly knew what to say. She had never in all of her years of churchgoing heard anything like that. Could it be that this remarkable young man, so fearless and dependable, and yet so gentle and understanding, had something that her minister at home had never known? Could it be that that was why she had noticed the lack of bitterness in his tone and his face when Richard had spoken so slurringly back there in the drug store? If that was true, everything in life could be different!

She was silent, deep in thought as they drove the last block and parked in front of Snellers' house. Roger waited for her to speak.

"You mean," she asked him wonderingly, "that if I take this trouble as something God has planned for me, instead of fighting it and fuming, then I might get to know Him a little better and I might be more like Him when it's over?"

He turned and looked at her with a solemn smile.

"That's exactly what I mean!" he said with authority in his tone as if he spoke from a depth of experience.

"But how—why, I don't see how I'm going to *stand* it!" she cried under her breath, as if the Snellers might even then be listening to what she said. "You don't know! We don't have *one thing* in common! Oh, I feel like a heel for talking this way, but it's—it's really—impossible!"

He smiled again but there was no softening, no deviation in his manner from the truth he had stated.

"But our God is the God of the Impossible!" he reminded her. "*You* couldn't stand it, neither could I. But *He* can. Think what the Lord Jesus had to stand when He was here. And He did stand it with sweetness and gentleness, and brought Life whereever He went. All of the power He had is ours, His very nature has been made over to 'every one that believeth.' If you are truly His child, by faith in His death for you, you can draw on that power of His. It's like making out a check on an unlimited bank account. And it *works!* I *know*. He will not let you down."

There was a quiet triumphant ring to Roger's voice and Wynelle felt her eyes drawn to his face again. Once more she was aware of the inner goodness of this boy. She wondered about how great were the things he must have suffered, to be able to speak with assurance like this. With sudden insight she knew that she would never really get to know him until she too had suffered.

"I'll be talking to Him about you," he assured her, "as I have ever since you jumped from the plane, and I'll ask Him to make it all plain to you. Do you have a Bible with you?"

Wynelle's face grew red in the darkness.

"Why, I have—I have a little book of verses I like to read. But no, I had so little room I didn't bring the whole Bible. I suppose they have one at Snellers', though." She felt very small.

But there was no condemnation in his tone as Roger said:

"I'll hunt one up for you, and mark some places to read. And I'll be in tomorrow to see how you are. Cheer up, kid. You may think you can't take it, but you'll be like the little boy who told his mother, 'Maw, I thought when the dentist pulled my tooth that I was a-goin' ta die, but just afore I did, the thing come out!'"

Wynelle laughed heartily and the laughing relaxed her.

But it stirred up hatred in the heart of the boy within the house who was listening as they came up the walk. So his cousin had ditched him in favor of a murderer's son, had she? Well, that fellow would find out that he couldn't walk off with his date right from under his nose that way!

When Wynelle's professionally bandaged foot came into view, Richard still glowered sullenly in the background.

"Gosh, I didn't know you wanted to go to a doctor, Nellie," he blustered. "You said your foot was all right!"

But nobody paid much attention to him.

Alberta dropped her knitting and cried, "Oh how *terrible!* What has happened? Oh, I don't know *where* we can put you! Shouldn't you go to the hospital?"

She pranced around wringing her hands, while Roger stood gravely holding Wynelle in the middle of the living room, as tenderly as if she were a baby.

Cousin Dick was not home yet, but Mona appeared at sound of the hubbub and announced: "Oh for pity's sake, mom, cut the racket. Bring her in here where she belongs. I'll have to put up with it, I guess. There's nothing else to do."

Roger's face grew more and more stern as he followed Mona down the short hallway to her room and placed Wynelle gently on the bed. The others were crowding around, so there was no chance for him to speak a reassuring word to her alone.

Thelma remained somewhat aloof from them all, looking sardonic as usual. Richard did not even come into the room.

Only Della showed some sympathy.

"Oh gee, Wyn, that's tough!" she commiserated. "And I was counting on you to go out with me tomorrow to play tennis at the club. You said you could play, and I thought we'd try you out. If you were good enough I was going to let you play in our mixed doubles next week. Mary Lee is sick." Wynelle only groaned with pain.

It was Roger who thought to draw a blanket over her and stopped her as she tried to take off the sweater he had loaned her.

"Keep it now," he said, leaning over to tuck the blanket about her. "I won't need it and you must be kept warm. I'll stop in tomorrow, but you be sure to send for me if there is anything *at all* that I can do for you!"

He gave her a steady look that was a command and withdrew but Wynelle called after him, "I'll see you tomorrow. Perhaps I can thank you more intelligently then." She gave a shaky little laugh.

She had a feeling that Roger understood that she would like to say more but didn't feel free to. Roger understood so much without telling! That was a great comfort. She did not know how heavy his heart was with compassion for the girl who seemed to be tossed so casually into the midst of people who were utterly uncongenial.

"Lord, meet her need. Give her real victory there!" He found himself praying earnestly as he got into his car and drove home. He could guess what a night of misery Wynelle would have to spend.

And he was not mistaken. The pain in her foot was continual agony, and she could not turn from side to side at all. Mona's heavy snores did not help her weary nerves, and every time Mona moved the bed covers pulled on her foot and gave it a fresh thrust of pain, until finally Wynelle struggled until she loosened the covers from the foot of the bed entirely. Then Mona awoke and complained crossly that she was cold.

Wynelle thought that the night would never end. She scarcely slept at all and when she did fall into a restless doze, she thought that all the Snellers were about her pulling at the bandage on her foot and insisting that she get up and play tennis in the front yard of her new house, that she would lose it if she did not. Over and over she dreamed that with variations. Sometimes Roger was her partner in the game, but just as he would be about to hit the winning stroke he would disappear and Richard would take his place. Yet all the night long she was aware of Someone standing near her just out of sight, Someone who had offered to help her; Someone with a strong gentle look like Roger's, but it wasn't Roger. She would turn and try to see Him, but she never could. It was not until near dawn that the delirium subsided and she fell asleep.

Fortunately Dick and Alberta's room was on the other side of the house from hers, or she would have heard their conversation when Dick came in and heard the news of her accident.

Dick swore with heat. But Alberta turned on him.

"Well, this is all your fault," she blamed him. "You *would* have me invite the girl here. How do you think *I* like it, to have an invalid to wait on? I declare, it seems as if there was no end to the things I have to put up with. And I'm not the only one. Poor Mona can't get away from it. Really, what that child has suffered already in her short life!" Alberta shed a few tears.

"Oh can the water works!" stormed Dick. "There's more to it than a little inconvenience. I'm up against it for cash right now, and I've been counting on making something from the sale of her house. Now if she puts her foot down and won't sell it, I'm sunk. Why, I can't even raise the money to pay my secretary pretty soon, if things don't break for me! There's only one chance of my pulling out of this mess, and that is if I can land that Commonwealth Attorney job. Johnson, the C.A. that's been there for years is retiring, definitely. I'm not sure just when, but soon. That could be a break for me."

There was a harassed edge to Dick's voice and he yanked at his collar button until it gave and rolled away under the bureau. He swore again.

"Well, you don't need to take it out on me!" whined Alberta. "I don't see what I could do about it. I gave up two whole days to take the girl around, just laying aside everything I had planned to do, to please you."

"Is that so!" he turned on her in fury. "Who do you think I'm trying to earn money for, I ask you? And after all, she is your relative, remember!"

Dick flung himself out of the room and into the bathroom, leaving Alberta to cry herself to sleep before he returned.

In the morning he knocked on the door downstairs before Mona was awake.

"I'll have to see Wynelle," he called. "Hurry, for I mustn't be late."

There was fretting and fussing a moment and Mona opened the door, her kimono slung haphazardly about her. Wynelle lay white and worn amid the disarray of early morning, too spent with the pain and fever of the night to care whether she was presentable or not.

Dick tried to be pleasant.

"Too bad you hurt your foot," he said hurriedly. "Do you think you won't be able to go down to the office with me?"

Wynelle shook her head wearily.

"No, I'm sure I couldn't. The doctor told me it might make a lot of trouble later if I don't stay off of it now. I'm sorry I'm going to be laid up here, to be a bother to you all. I'll try not to make any more trouble than necessary." She managed a weak little smile.

"Oh, don't concern yourself about that," he said. "Alberta and the girls can look after you all right, and be glad to, I'm sure!" he lied. "I guess, then, the best thing to do is to bring those people up here this morning. I'll have all the preliminaries over with down at the office and all in the world you will have to do is sign your name. I guess that won't bother your foot too much?"

Wynelle closed her eyes as if to draw from an unseen source the courage to meet this insistent man.

"But I told you last night that I don't wish to sell my house," she said patiently.

"Oh, come now, don't let's go into all that again. I thought I had made plain to you that it's really the only wise thing to do. Besides," he took a step nearer to her bed as if to speak confidentially, "I'll have to admit that if you back out now you'll put me on the spot. I've given them my word that they could have it right away. I'm sure you wouldn't want me to go back on my word for just a whim, now would you?"

His voice was rough and rasping, and jarred on Wynelle's worn nerves. She summoned all her strength again.

"I'm sorry, Dick, but I never said that I would sell the house, and after all, it is mine to dispose of. I dislike to take this attitude especially when you have been so kind as to invite me here as your guest, and you can realize, I'm sure, that I feel all the more uncomfortable about crossing your advice now that I am laid up like this in your home, but I *do not wish* to sell at present!"

With great difficulty Dick restrained his anger.

"Young lady," he said, "I'm sure when you realize what you are doing, you will be sorry for such a foolish move."

He was about to continue with his argument when the front doorbell rang and, this being the one morning a week when the colored maid was there, she opened the door and admitted Roger Blackstone bearing a florist's box.

"She's in there," she told him pointing, and in a moment Roger appeared at the bedroom door behind Cousin Dick.

"Good morning," greeted Roger cheerily. "How're you doin'?" He smiled at Wynelle first and turning, nodded politely to Mr. Sneller. "Good morning, sir," he said, putting out his hand.

Mr. Sneller looked at the hand and then glared at Roger.

"May I ask," he blazed, "by what right you come barging into my house at this hour in the morning? Or at any time, for that matter?"

Roger's face went white but he looked Mr. Sneller steadily in the eye.

"I came to inquire about Miss Williams and bring her flowers," he said in an even tone.

"Oh?" sneered Mr. Sneller. "Since when does a florist's delivery boy feel it necessary to bring his goods into the sick room?"

Roger swallowed hard and then smiled.

"Well," he said merrily as if Mr. Sneller had been joking with him, "them was my orders, sir!"

"You and your flowers can get out of here, young fellow, and don't you ever dare to set foot in my house again. You are definitely *not* welcome!"

"Oh!" cried Wynelle in a hurt voice. She had listened in incredulous horror to the scene between the two men. "Dick, you don't understand. Roger is my friend! He saved my life! I'm glad to see him, and I *want* my flowers!" She tried to rise up but she fell back and moaned.

"Oh-h-h?" jeered Dick. "So *he's* the nigger in the woodpile, is he? Well, I'll take care he keeps his dirty hands out of here and out of your business after this. Now get out!"

Trembling with anger and chagrin, Wynelle gazed wide-eyed at Roger as if surely he would do something to straighten out this awful situation.

But he looked steadily at Dick for a moment and then he looked back at Wynelle with tender sympathy as if to say, "I know just how hard all this is for you!" Then he spoke to her: "Cheer up, kid, and don't worry about me. Let me know if there's anything I can do for you." He took her cold trembling little hand in his and gave her a warm firm clasp and a radiant smile, and then with one more steady look at Dick walked out of the house.

Wynelle turned her head and covering her face with the pillow she burst into heartbroken sobs.

Her cousin stood in perplexed anger another moment, and then he said to the pillow, "Come, come now, Wynelle, don't be so upset. If you knew all that I know about this young scamp you wouldn't have anything to do with him. It's really a good thing that I was here and discovered that he has been trying to be friendly with you, for of course you wouldn't know that he is not a person for you to make friends with. Now I tell you what we'll do. I'll just put off the buyers as best I can this morning, and perhaps another day you will feel better and we can go all over the matter and straighten it out. Don't worry about it now."

He went out and Wynelle was left to herself for Mona had departed when the scene first began.

When she could control her indignation and her sobs enough she reached for the box and opened it. With tender fingers she drew back the green wax paper and caught her breath at the loveliness there. Yellow roses they were, bright as the sunshine had been the day before on the lawn of her little house. She buried her hot face in them and drank in the fragrance. How inexpressibly sweet it was that they should come to her now! Then she saw the card nestled in among the greenery. She drew it out of the little envelope and read, "Yours because of His Cross, Roger." Her heart filled with awe.

Did he mean that the roses were hers, or he was hers? Well, whichever he meant, it was sweet. A thrill shot through her. It was sweet but terribly bitter, too, as she realized that she might never get to see Roger again. He must be hurt and angry at Dick, and to think that she had just lain there and scarcely said a word in defense of Roger! That seemed inexcusable to her. She felt that she did not deserve such a friend if she could not stand up for him. She had been too stunned at her cousin's insulting talk to think what she should say or do. After all, she was Cousin Dick's guest and he had a right to forbid anyone his house if he pleased. She writhed to think that she was imprisoned here. Frantically she tried to think of a way that she could secure a room somewhere else. But how could she find one now, crippled as she was? She could not bring herself to ask Alberta to hunt one, and besides that wouldn't be right, to tell her hostess that she couldn't stand her house any longer!

She thought of asking Roger if he would look her up a place, but then if she did have a room, she couldn't take care of herself yet, not until she could get around better. Besides, if she wasn't working, her money would soon be gone, and then she would have to come running back to Snellers', which would be far more unpleasant than staying here a little longer now.

So she reasoned around and around in circles until she was weary.

WYNELLE LAY A long time weeping and trying to pray, and wondering what she ought to do next. She was stunned with the shock of hearing her cousin insult the man who had done so much for her. Yet try as she would she could not shut out entirely the haunting fear lest she might be wrong herself in her estimate of Roger. After all, she knew so little of him; these people had lived there in the same town with him all their lives. Could it be that he had done something dishonorable? Was it possible that he was in some vague way, she could not imagine how, trying to misrepresent the house situation to her?

She made an honest attempt to face the matter squarely, putting out of the question the fact that she did not like her relatives one little bit. She admitted to herself that they could be right about Roger, even though she did not like them, personally. She had to confess to herself that she did not want them to be right. Very much she wanted them to be wrong, because she had an almost impossibly high ideal of this young man, and she could not bear to have it spoiled. She did not imagine herself in love with him. That was ridiculous, of course. Why, she scarcely knew him. But everything about him, great or small, that she had observed so far was in his favor.

At last, weary with her wondering and reasoning, she bethought her of her little book of Bible verses. She had not read in it since she came, for she had had it packed in one of her suitcases and those had been in the plane. When she brought them in yesterday she had taken out the few dresses she thought she would need and slid the bags just as they were under her side of the bed, for Mona had made no provision for her to use any more space than the one little drawer that she had offered on arrival. She remembered having seen the little book when she had taken out her dresses. It was tucked in the side pocket of the smaller of the two bags. If only she could reach it! She had a feeling that she might find in it the help that she so sorely needed just now. She had not forgotten what Roger had told her about her Heavenly Father caring for her, even though she did not deserve His care. She would try to draw on that Heavenly "bank account" now, she decided. For she felt more than ever alone now that the one person who seemed to be a true friend had been denied the right to come and see her.

Slowly, painfully, she edged herself sideways so that she could touch the catch of the bag. Every time she moved her ankle gave another sickening twinge, but she kept on trying and reaching. She had to stop and rest every few minutes, for she was weak from the pain and the strain of the horrid scene in her room that morning.

At last she managed to open the catches and reached into the front corner of the bag. Yes, there was the little book. She could feel its rounded leather edges. She drew it out carefully lest she tear the pages, and then she clicked shut one of the catches again.

She closed her eyes for an instant before she opened the book to the date of the day.

"Please, oh God, speak to me somehow, now. I need You so very much. I don't know why I should be here, all alone! But I do want to learn about the Cross, and all that Roger was talking about."

She was not a superstitious person, but she had a feeling that a God who cared as Roger said He did would hear her plea in her great need. She opened her eyes and read:

"Lo, I am with you always, even unto the end of the world."

A rush of grateful tears blinded her eyes so that she could not read on for some minutes. To think that this of all the hundreds of verses in the Bible, should be at the head of the page for that particular day! Surely God had answered. He *did* care.

She wiped her eyes on the edge of the sheet and went on, eagerly, as if listening for a loved voice.

"God is our refuge and strength, a very present help in trouble."

Again the tears came. It was too wonderful, these assurances of His nearness and His help. She felt as if a great load had been lifted from her heart. She had supposed that possibly there would be some word of rebuke for her wilfulness in coming east, or for her long neglect of God's interests. But there was nothing but love and care and assurance. She read on.

"Beloved," Oh, how sweet that was to her heart! "Beloved, think it not strange concerning the fiery trial that is to try you, as though some strange thing happened unto you—" Why! that was exactly what she had been thinking, that all this was so strange! And she had been on the verge of blaming God for letting it all happen to *her*. "But rejoice—" Yesterday she would have said that was impossible, but now she began to have a glimmer of understanding of how even a trial such as she was called to go through, could be a cause for rejoicing, for already she had been drawn closer to her Saviour than she had ever felt before.

"Rejoice, inasmuch as ye are partakers of Christ's sufferings." Oh, that must have some reference to the work of the Cross in her life. Roger had mentioned that. It was still all very strange to her untaught soul, but she felt as if she were touching eternal things, unseen but all the more real for that, things that would mean more to her than earthly life or even death. She was fairly breathless as she read on to the end of the little page. There were references for each verse, but she had no Bible. How she wished she could look them up and read the context. But she knew that she had been strengthened already and she closed the book and gave thanks.

Just then Mona returned. The family had had breakfast some time ago, but it had just occurred to Alberta that Wynelle might like something to eat. She had sent Mona in with a cup of coffee and a couple of pieces of toast. Mona had slopped the coffee over into the saucer on the way, but Wynelle smiled and thanked her for the food.

Mona tried in her way to make up for the scene her father had made.

"Don't let dad's raging worry you too much," she told Wynelle disparagingly. "I never do. I always let him rave and then do as I please. Of course I must say I don't envy your choice of boy friends, but everyone to his taste, I always say, and if you're in love with a guy, you want him, that's all there is to it! So go ahead with the Blackstone boy if you like. Nobody can stop you, and I won't tell on you."

A tumult of indignation began to well up in Wynelle's breast. What right had this unspeakable girl to link her name with Roger's? She was incensed that Mona would dare to talk in that vulgar way! She was just about to blaze out at her when all of a sudden she seemed to see Roger's white face, with the steady look that he had cast on Dick Sneller when he had insulted him. Why hadn't Roger raged at Dick? Was that another fiery trial? Something that Roger had learned to rejoice over, or at least to overlook? Wynelle closed her lips and said nothing.

"Oh my!" rattled on Mona. "Flowers, eh? Getting kind of serious, I should say, when they bring you flowers at eight o'clock in the morning. Open them up and let's have a look. What are they, orchids? Too bad if they are and you can't go out anywhere to sport them."

Wynelle had closed the box carefully to keep in the freshness of the flowers until she could get them into water. Reluctantly she opened the box for she did not relish having this girl maul over her flowers. They seemed almost sacred.

"Whew! Aren't they lush! Gee, if a guy sent me those I wouldn't care if his father was a murderer. You marry the man, anyway, not his father. That's the mistake I made the first time.

Too much family on his side. I won't try that again. Thank heaven Emory Ames has no family—not in evidence, anyway. If he has he pays no attention to them, and that's a lot better. You go your way and let the rest go theirs. Less battling. What a two years I put through! Wow! Say, you want these in some water, don't you!" She started to take them away but Wynelle stopped her. She had a feeling she could not trust her beloved flowers out of her sight.

"Oh, if you will just bring me a vase or something, I'll fix them. I don't want to bother you. I know I'm going to be terribly in your way, Mona, and I'm sorry."

Mona looked at her with surprise and shrugged.

"Gee, don't think a thing of it. You won't be much in the way. I'm not one for fussing around a sickroom, I'll go my own way, but don't you worry. I can take it if you can."

With that meagre assurance, Mona marched off and returned with a Mason jar of water.

"This isn't very beautiful," she admitted sourly, "but it's all I could find. Lizzie is scrubbing the pantry floor and I can't get in where the vases are."

"Oh, that will be all right," replied Wynelle, relieved to have anything at all, although it seemed almost sacrilegious to put those gorgeous roses into a mere preserving jar. Still, after she had arranged them carefully they seemed to glorify the jar.

"I suppose," thought Wynelle to herself, "that is something like what Roger meant yesterday, when he said we have to die to self to let Jesus Christ be seen." Again she was aware of that Presence, not behind her now, in patient rejection, but somewhere nearer than that, within her perhaps, and she knew that wherever He was, He was glad because of her, and joy sprang into her heart.

She was alone most of that day. Part of the time she slept. Once or twice Alberta came to the door, but Wynelle preferred to pretend to be asleep even when she was not, for she did not feel up to talking to her yet.

Thelma walked past the door once, and primly asked how she felt. Della, pretty in her new sport outfit, poked her head in the door and said, "Sorry you can't make it. Hope you're feeling better. Some other time we'll try you out."

But no one seemed to feel the necessity of asking whether they could do anything for her. Not that she wanted them to. She was far more content to be left alone than to have to feel that she was a burden to them. Still, it did seem rather friendless and lonely. At first when the wonder of the message she had found in her little book was still fresh in her mind, she was able to overlook the neglect and the loneliness, but late in the afternoon, when her fever started to rise a little and her foot ached unbelievably, she began to feel sorry for herself again, and she writhed in her soul with the torment of having to stay here in this house where she was so obviously unwelcome.

Then she got to thinking what a nice time she would have had to look forward to that evening. She had been so eager for that ride with Roger. And he had promised to talk over the house situation with her, and also that other wonderful matter of the meaning of the Cross. With the remembrance of that she felt suddenly ashamed of herself and she took a deep breath and closed her eyes, trying to feel for the Presence who had been with her that morning. A measure of her peace returned and she bravely tried to smile when Alberta came to her door with a bite of supper.

"I'm so sorry," Wynelle said, "that I'm making you all this trouble. Surely after a few days I will be able to get around a little. And until then I wish you would let me do some mending or something. I'm sure that there must be things like that I could do to help you. I really don't want to be a burden."

"Oh, you don't need to feel that way," said Alberta coldly. "I do think Dick was quite upset this morning because you seem to think *you* are more capable than *he* is of handling your business. I'm sure I don't know why people will go to doctors when they are sick, but don't have *sense* enough to go to lawyers when it's a case of law or something like that. But of course," she spoke piously, "it's your own property to do as you please with. I suppose you have some of your grandmother in you. She always *was* so stubborn and thought she knew more than anybody else."

Wynelle winced with pain as she tried to raise herself on one elbow and reach the tray to put it down beside her on the bed. She felt as if there were no use in trying to be pleasant and helpful to these people. They seemed to be bent on misjudging her. She made a little attempt to laugh off Alberta's remark.

"Well, maybe I am like my grandmother," she said. "I've always been told that I looked like her. To tell you the truth, I've always been pleased at that. I never saw my grandmother since I was a tiny thing, but I have seen pictures of her and I always thought she was sweet."

"That's what *some* people thought," admitted Alberta acidly. "They didn't have to *live* with her, or at least in the same town with her and try to guide her into *sensible* ways of doing."

Wynelle felt unfit to cope with that sentiment and let the subject drop, and she was relieved when Alberta went out of the room again and left her alone.

The family were still at supper and she could hear them talking, bickering as usual over nothing, occasionally bringing her name into the conversation in a lowered tone, when the doorbell rang again.

For a glad instant Wynelle thought that possibly Roger was going to defy Mr. Sneller's prohibition and come to see her anyway, but she knew immediately that that would not be like Roger. If he knew he was not wanted he would never intrude himself, she was sure.

Wynelle could hear Della go to the door. A high-pitched voice that sounded like a little boy said with carefully schooled accent: "Would you please give this to Miss Williams. Thanks! 'by."

Della laughed at the small messenger who had evidently disappeared on the instant his last word was out. Wynelle wondered what could be his errand, when Della appeared at her door and handed her a square package.

"For you, Wyn," she told her unceremoniously and tossed the package onto the bed. "Hope it's candy!" She laughed and went out.

Wonderingly Wynelle untied the string. There was no name or writing of any kind on the parcel.

She worked swiftly, lest some of the family come in on her before she had the pleasure of the gift to herself. They always seemed to be able to say the very thing that would hurt the most.

There was a plain white box inside the wrappings, and when she lifted the lid, there was a book. It was bound in soft dark blue leather, and the edges and lettering were gold. "HOLY BIBLE" was stamped on the back, and underneath it said, "With Notes for Young Christians." With a little cry of delight Wynelle seized it, hugging it to her, loving the very smell and feel of the limp leather. The pages fell open of themselves to a place near the middle of the book and there was an envelope with her name on it.

She recognized the handwriting instantly, and slipped the letter under her pillow, for she heard someone coming. She had no desire to have to share her precious letter from Roger. She was sure now that they must be wrong. How could she have doubted him?

It was Della and Richard who came barging in.

"We came for some candy," cried Della. "Come on now, don't be stingy!" She reached for the white box.

But Wynelle, her face wreathed in happy smiles only laughed.

"Why surely," she assented, "I'll share what I have with you. Listen to this!" She dropped her eyes to the Book and her eye fell on a place which was neatly underlined. Wonderingly she read, "Thy words were found and I did eat them." She gave a gasp of amazement. "Oh!" she cried, and went on: " 'Thy word was to me the joy and rejoicing of my heart.' Well," she exclaimed in obvious surprise, "what do you think of that! It *was* something to eat! Isn't that wonderful?"

Della and Richard only stood and stared at her.

"Isn't *what* wonderful?" asked Richard phlegmatically. "Sounds like church to me. Ye gods! What on earth is that book? The Bible? Let me out of here."

He promptly left the room but Della stayed a moment and studied Wynelle with a puzzled expression.

"Say, you know you *are* different," she said again. "I thought so the first time I saw you and now I know you are. I don't know whether you're screwy or whether you've got something. But I'm inclined to like you. Say, didn't you really get any candy?"

"No," smiled Wynelle, "something a lot sweeter. Would you like to hear some more? I don't really know where to start to read yet, but I'm going to learn. Maybe you would like to read with me sometimes?" She put the question timidly, half hoping that Della would refuse, for she thought she would rather enjoy her new treasure all by herself.

But Della said, "Thanks no. I never read anything if I can help it. There's too much else that's interesting to do. Well, I got a date. So long."

Strangely enough Wynelle felt a keen disappointment that Della did not want to stay and read with her. She was surprised at the feeling. She found herself thinking how different Della could be if she wanted to.

She turned back to her Bible then and read snatches here and there, and one by one she could hear the family go out on their various appointments. She was glad they were gone. When she was sure she was alone she took out her letter.

CHAPTER 12

WYNELLE'S EYES FAIRLY devoured each word.

"Dear Sky Rider," he began, and she gave a little crooked smile.

"It is a keen disappointment to me not to be able to come to see you, especially now that you are laid up and in no pleasant situation, I am sure. What I would like to do is to barge in there and carry you off to some quiet place of refuge where you would have loving care. But I have no right to do that. My hands are tied and I can't help but feel that it is God who has tied them. When and if He unties them, believe me, I'll be right there on the job! Till then, if you need anything or there is anything you would like me to do for you, write me a note and slip it under the edge of the screen in your window. I'm up before it's light and I will find it.

"I can't blame the Snellers for feeling as they do about me. Besides the fact of my father's disgrace, I pulled a pretty mean trick on them one Halloween night when I was just a kid and although I have since apologized, they have never forgotten it. I'm ashamed to say that it still seems funny to me! But I had no business to do it. I didn't know the Lord very well then, and I still felt pretty bitter about Mr. Sneller's part in what happened to my father.

"I hope you will like the Bible 'enclosed herewith.' I sure did enjoy getting it for you. I like this new edition because the notes help if you don't have anyone around to explain the text.

"When you are able to be out again, I hope we'll have many an hour together. Till then I'll be praying for your speedy recovery, and still more earnestly for the Lord's own blessing and victory for you.

> Sincerely yours because of the Cross,
> Roger."

Wynelle's eyes were starry with wonder when she finished that letter. No boy had ever written to her like that before. It seemed to speak to her from a high place to which she felt she never could attain, yet at the same time it was so human, so boyish, so warm and friendly. To think that a man like that should be even a little bit interested in her! Yet he had cared enough to remember her even though her own relatives had insulted him.

She fingered the handsome leather of the Bible, delighting in the soft tissue-thin India pages. The notes at the bottom of each page fascinated her. Her heart swelled with gratitude, and she could not help a little extra feeling of delight that this young man had shown such good taste in his selection of the finest of bindings. Then she glanced lovingly at her flowers, beside her on the window sill. The heavy golden buds had started to open and show their hearts to her. How she rejoiced in them. Then she turned to her letter once more and read it over and over.

At last she closed her eyes, folding her hands close over the letter that lay on her breast.

"Oh God," she prayed softly, "You have given me *so* much! More than I ever asked or thought of asking. I want to go on and be *some* good to You here. Please show me how, and bless Roger! Amen!"

And it was not until the middle of the night when she lay awake thinking it all over that she realized that she had learned to rejoice a little in her fiery trial!

But the days were not all full of delight by any means. Wynelle was left to take care of her own foot most of the time, except when the doctor came in a time or two to inspect it. And while the family did bring her food, it was carelessly prepared, and sometimes because they forgot her for such long periods, she was actually hungry. But at such times she would take out her letters and read them over. For Roger wrote every day, sometimes answering question she had asked in the letters she slipped under the screen, sometimes enclosing a page of jokes he had cut out of a magazine. And then she had her Bible, too. She spent hours studying and drinking in truths that she had never understood before. She learned more of spiritual truths in those days than she had in all her life before.

She did the family mending, and when she was able to sit up, even took some dictation for Cousin Dick using a portable typewriter which he brought from the office one day. He had been careful not to mention the house again, for he was keen enough to realize that he would defeat his own purpose if he forced the issue too quickly.

He was delighted with her stenography.

"Well say," he exclaimed, "why couldn't you help us out at the office? You do as good work as the girl we have had, and she is so undependable I've been thinking of letting her go. Would you like the job? You say you feel as if you'd like to do something to pay your way here," he gave a little shrug, "why not work for me? Then you could stay right on here. Of course I'd pay you a little something besides, so you would feel as if you're making something."

"Oh!" cried Wynelle, half delighted and half apprehensive at the idea of working for Cousin Dick. "Why, I—I hadn't even decided whether I'm going to remain in the east or not." She wanted to give herself time to think. She had not the slightest desire to stay at the Snellers', but could it be that God still wanted her here? In any case, it would be the cheapest way for her to live, and she did want very much to repay the Snellers in some way, if only so that she need not feel obligated to them. For when she was up and around she fully intended to choose her own friends, and

Roger Blackstone would be one of them. She would not feel right about remaining at Snellers' indefinitely if she did that, but the offer did seem like a way out for her at present.

So she promised to think it over.

It was two days after she was hurt, and she had written her first little note to Roger thanking him with all her heart for the Bible and his letter, when she awoke in the early morning and saw outside the window close by her bed a scarlet geranium nodding at her as if in gay greeting. With a soft exclamation of delight she lifted the screen, cautiously lest she awaken Mona. Its pot was set in a chubby little hand-painted jug of dark green and soft yellows. There were several buds on the plant, giving promise of days of brightness for her. Well she knew from whom it came. Roger's thoughtfulness continually amazed her. Before she left Uniontown she had not believed that there was in the world such a boy as he. She gave her head a little shake to try to cast off the constant thoughts of him that kept twining themselves about her heart. If she was not careful she was going to fall head over heels in love with him, and wouldn't *that* be a fine situation to be in! For she persuaded herself a dozen times a day and many times at night, that Roger was simply being kind to a poor lonely person who, he saw, had no friends. That would be like him. He wasn't trying to be a lover. At least he didn't act like any boys who had ever tried to make love to her. She admitted to herself that she liked Roger's ways far better than the others', but he was not mushy, she decided, and he would not like it if he thought that she was thinking more of him than she would of any ordinary friend. So she struggled to keep her thinking on a sane basis and thank him simply and straightforwardly for all that he had done for her.

But Mona would not let her alone.

"Well, for cryin' out loud!" she exclaimed when she saw the geranium. "Where did you get that thing! Gosh, I don't know how you do it! You've been here in town only a little while and you get more flowers and presents than I do. And you're such a quiet mousey little thing, too. What have you got that I don't have?"

She said it in a half-laughing, half-envious tone.

Wynelle chuckled gaily.

"I have a sprained ankle right now! Want it?"

"Thanks, no!" Mona made a sour face. "I'm sure if I did have it I couldn't be half as cheerful as you are about it. I'll have to hand you that! I don't know how you do it."

Wynelle could have wept for joy, but she only said,

"*I* couldn't, myself. I found that out. I must admit that I didn't feel very cheerful about the whole thing. It isn't fun to be beholden to people you don't know very well, even if they are relatives." She smiled. "I just had to ask the Lord to do what I couldn't do," she added shyly.

"Humph!" grunted Mona unbelievingly. "I don't know why you'd even *want* to be cheerful. I'm sure I wouldn't. I'd just like to take it out on everybody all the time!"

Wynelle wondered what to say to that. She found herself longing to help this girl.

"Well I guess I had to ask Him for even the 'wanting,'" she confessed. "I'm finding out that He does whatever we really want Him to do."

"Humph!" responded Mona again. "Well, it's too deep for me. I'm goin' to get breakfast. Anything you want?"

Wynelle was touched. That was the first time Mona had even thought to ask what she would like.

"No thanks," she said brightly. "I'm quite all right. The doctor said I might get up and struggle around a little today."

" 'sgood," replied Mona. "If you get a chance would you mind mending my nylon evening slip? I tore it last night at the dance."

"I'll be glad to," said Wynelle. "Just lay it out."

Mona gave her another puzzled sidelong glance as she laid it out on the bed, and then went out.

She had scarcely shut the door after her when she poked her head in again and said irrelevantly, "You know Dell thinks you're really something on a stick! You should have heard her rave about you to Nancy Gilkie last night. That's a lot for Dell. She thinks she's hard-boiled."

She closed the door and went on, but Wynelle could hardly keep back tears of joy. How marvelously God had answered the desire of her heart. A short time ago she would never have dreamed that she could care whether these girls liked her or not. And what had she done? Nothing. Oh, she had filled in her time by mending their hose and their torn garments. But the joy she was receiving in return far outweighed the little effort she had put on serving them. Roger surely had taught her the way of peace and joy! What a man he was. And how she longed to have another talk with him. As soon as she could that day she wrote him a little note telling him of her conversation with Mona. She knew that she could count on him to share her joy in it.

Every morning there was some token of Roger's care for her on the window sill. Sometimes it was a letter, sometimes a few flowers, once it was a box of delicious homemade chocolate peppermints. "A friend of mine makes these. Hope you like 'em!" said a note in the box.

And the morning of the day that she was to be allowed to put her foot down she discovered a long slender package on the sill and in it were two curiously fashioned canes. A note tied to them said, "The doc says you're able to use these now. I'm glad." It seemed that there was nothing he didn't think to do for her!

It was toward the end of the third week that she was at last able to be about the house. She was beginning to hope that before long she could get outside, for then she could have the ride that Roger had promised so long ago.

On Friday morning she found a little flat square package at her window.

It turned out to be an exquisite hand-painted motto framed in

silver which said, "Beloved, think it not strange . . . but rejoice!" She had written Roger about finding that verse in her
little book the morning after he had been ordered out of the
house. It was precious to have him remind her of it in this way.
She couldn't help wondering if he meant anything special by
that "Beloved" and then she tried to persuade herself that of
course he didn't, that was just the way the verse started. Anyway
it was lovely.

There was a short note in the box, too. It said:

"By the time you get this I'll be a thousand miles away, but I'll
be meeting you at the Throne. '*He* hath said, I will never leave
thee nor forsake thee!'

"I have a tough job to do which may mean a very great deal
to me in more ways than one. I would appreciate prayer. Maybe
we can have that ride when I get back."

Wynelle hugged that note to her heart. She was aghast at how
much she dreaded the thought that Roger would not be in town
through the coming days. Not that she ever saw him. She had
stayed awake many a time to try to discover when it was that he vis-
ited her window sill, but she had never caught him at it. Yet now
just the idea that he would not be coming, and that if there were
a need she could not let him know of it, made her feel terribly
alone. She had not realized how much she had learned to depend
upon him.

But she took another look at the lovely little blue and silver
motto and set her lips firmly to trust and wait. She knew that she
would not be alone now. Roger's God was her God, and that
meant everything.

CHAPTER 13

THE NEXT DAY was Saturday. In Chicago it was windy and sullen. The gusts seemed to take sudden fits of anger and burst upon the city unexpectedly, whipping an awning from its frame or slapping wet sheets of newspaper into a pedestrian's face. The summer was scarcely past but the rain that lashed whole sections of the city was like a fall rain. People on the streets looked chagrined, then annoyed, then indignant and finally discouraged to think that the elements should so take advantage of them at this time of year.

A slender woman hurried nervously down the street, her damp skirts flapping dismally about her. Her thin shoulders stooped badly. Her black coat, handsome and stylish years ago, was threadbare. Her black shoes, evidently selected at one time to display the pretty curve of her instep, were worn down to a rakish angle at the heel. A silk scarf of fine quality, but frayed at the corners, covered her graying hair. There was a discouraged droop to her whole body as she turned in at the back door of a second-rate restaurant.

She shook her coat, annoyed at finding how wet it was, hung it up on a hook which was already crowded, and nodded without smiling at a young waitress who slouched crossly into the kitchen with a tray. By force of habit she stepped to an ugly cracked mirror framed in brown chipped wood and began to work on her face. Her makeup was a pitiful attempt to hide the ravages of her nearly fifty years. Her eyes were dark blue and held a fascinating look of mystery, but her cheeks were fairly bony and her skin had that much-used look that comes of years of too many cosmetics. Her hair was still abundant, its original platinum blending well with the gray. She wore it smoothed back and coiled in a luxuriant knot. From behind it gave her a queenly appearance but that was contradicted by a full view of the anxious bitter lines of her face; they spoke of disappointment and frustration.

She tied on a big plastic apron and went to the sink, walking with an easy glide as if she still took for granted that she was attractive. A sniff, part of envy and part born of contempt, twisted the face of a homely old woman who was dishing up potatoes, but the woman paid no attention to it. Several other workers called a casual greeting but she merely nodded and went on with her work. Obviously she hated what she was doing but she doggedly persevered. Sometimes she would cast a frantic glance around as if she were considering escape from the drudgery, but her hands toiled on, held to her task by sheer necessity.

The day seemed unusually long because of the dreary weather. When at last it was over she took her disheartened lonely way back to her dismal little room in a shabby boarding house.

She had scarcely removed her wet coat when a knock sounded at her door. What could the landlady be wanting? Her rent was paid for the week. In some irritation she opened the door. A neatly dressed gentleman stood there with a printed form pad in his hand and a pencil poised.

"I'm sorry to bother you at night, madam," he apologized, "but I've stopped several times during the day and you were not in. I will not keep you. I am here only to ask you a few simple questions for our records. The council of churches—"

The woman interrupted him with an impatient wave of her hand and started to close the door.

"I am not interested in religion!" she stated with finality.

"Oh, we are not asking about your affiliations," pursued the visitor blandly. "The council of churches and the police department"—he made a mental note of the way her eyes came to attention when he mentioned the police department—"are co-operating in an effort to combat juvenile delinquency and forestall crime in the future generation. It is a question, you know," he continued rapidly in a singsong way as if he had made the same speech many times, "whether the Sunday Schools and churches are getting the results that might be expected. These questions I'd like to ask have only to do with whether you were a good little girl and went to Sunday School or not." He laughed disarmingly.

The woman shrugged.

"Oh, all right," she consented reluctantly. "But I'm tired and wet."

"Thank you," he smiled courteously. "I'll try not to keep you. Your name?"

"Myra Foster."

"*Mrs.* Myra Foster?" He raised his eyebrows and looked keenly at her.

She nodded.

"Mr. Foster is living?"

"N-no."

"Any children?"

She hesitated. "One," she answered mumblingly.

"Name?"

"Roger."

"Age?"

"Twenty—uh—four."

"He lives with you?"

"No."

"May I have his address, please?"

"I don't know it," she said rather crossly. The man looked up with surprise in his eyes. Resentfully Myra explained. "He was the son of a former marriage. He hasn't kept in touch with me."

"Oh, I see," replied her inquisitor impersonally. "Your former married name, please."

"Winters." She clipped off her answer as if she were annoyed at herself for having brought on more questions.

"And where were you living at the time you married Mr. Winters?"

"Seattle," she snapped.

"Your parents' name?" He continued unperturbed.

"Hibberd. But I can't see what that has to do with it." She was rapidly growing more indignant.

"Why," he explained gravely, "it was your parents, of course, who raised you. They would have to come into the picture. You were the only child?" His voice was smooth, and he did not appear to be watching her or taking any interest in her answers.

She flew into a rage. "I declare!" she stormed. "This country is getting to be as bad as Russia. I refuse to answer any more questions!" With that she slammed the door in his face and locked it.

But the man in the hallway was not at all upset by her actions. In fact he seemed quite pleased. He tucked his paper safely away into an inner pocket and departed.

He signaled a taxi and drove to a downtown office building where a light was still on. A tall lean young man was pacing up and down awaiting his return.

"Well, Blackstone," he said, flinging off his wet raincoat, "I found out quite a bit. For one thing, that mark on her wrist is there, just as you described."

Roger Blackstone gave a start and the lines of anxiety deepened in his face.

"There seems to be something cockeyed somewhere, though," went on the detective.

"There has been something very cockeyed for a long time," sighed Roger.

They sat down and talked it over. At last Roger reached for his coat.

"The catch seems to be whether she was an only child or not, as far as I can see," he concluded.

"Yes," agreed the other. "I think that's your clue."

"Well, I surely appreciate your help," said Roger putting out his hand in farewell. "I think I may be able to work out the rest of the problem now. What do I owe you, sir?"

"Oh, I'll send you a bill. It won't be too much. I'm glad to do anything I can for a friend of Ed. I think a lot of him."

Relieved in a measure, Roger thanked him and started home. Life looked very dark to him, but then it always had. And he was at last on the way to accomplish the thing that he had longed to do for years. His one desire since his father had been convicted had been to prove his innocence, and he was far nearer to that today than he had been.

He boarded his train eager to get back to his little brown home, and the charming owner of it. Her face had been before him constantly ever since the first day he had met her on the plane and she had bravely trusted him. He had never forgotten the sweetness of holding her so close to him, nor the thrill that shot through him the night of the accident when he had had the precious privilege of carrying her in his arms. She was so dainty, so exquisite, and yet so brave and straightforward. He could see her sweet brown eyes now, looking up trustfully at him. How he longed to take her in his arms in truth, and tell her that he loved her. But it was too soon; she would lose all trust in him if he did that. She could not possibly care for him as he did for her. Besides, there came again the old dark shadow of his disgrace. How could he ever ask a girl to share that with him? He sighed, shut his lips firmly and swallowed hard, turning his head aside, as if refusing a sweetmeat that tempted him strongly.

"Oh my Father," he murmured, closing his eyes wearily, "keep me from wanting anything I shouldn't have. And keep her in Your love and care! If I may not look after her, *You* do it, Lord! But somehow work out this whole tangle to Your glory!"

A peace settled on his face and he put his head back and began to piece together what he had learned. He knew that he was very near to proving what he had suspected for a long time.

CHAPTER 14

THAT SATURDAY HAD been an especially trying day for Wynelle. Her cousin, Dick, was cross in the morning and that started the whole family off on the wrong foot for the day.

Mona and Richard had a quarrel over who should have the car and their father ended up by refusing it to either of them, at which Richard swore terribly at his father and that made his mother cry.

Della seemed under great tension all day, excited and nervous, irritable when Wynelle did not fix her evening dress just as she wanted it. Dick left Wynelle a great pile of letters to address, gruffly telling her that he would expect her at the office Monday morning, that he had had to fire his secretary and he needed her immediately. Wynelle felt that she owed it to her relatives to go. Besides, while the doctor's bill had not been large, it had made one more inroad upon her pocketbook, and she had barely enough now to buy a ticket home if she did decide to return. She could not very well go about Maple Grove hunting a job, lame as she was, so this job seemed the only thing to do. But she was not eager over the prospect.

Alberta and Dick were out that evening, and only Thelma was left at home. She was almost always buried in a book or huddled at the radio. In spite of her pretense at intellectual heights, it was a little pathetic, thought Wynelle, to notice that her choice of radio programs was still quite childish.

Wynelle had finished the work they had left her, and seated on a stool, had helped Thelma with the supper dishes. They were in the two big chairs in the living room, Wynelle with her new

Bible and Thelma beside the radio, but she was staring fixedly at Wynelle rather then listening to her program.

Feeling her eyes upon her, Wynelle looked up with a smile. She had grown used to Thelma's gaze and she felt sorry for the girl for she really got very little attention from the rest of the family. She seemed to be just a tag-end of a child nobody cared for.

Thelma had a book in her lap as usual, but when Wynelle smiled at her a deep frown came over her face and she slammed the book shut and threw it fiercely on the floor.

Wynelle was surprised. Thelma did not generally break out in fits of anger. She usually kept a ridiculous dignity which was supposed to set her above the mundane affairs of her bourgeois family. Now two big tears rolled down her face which must have annoyed her to exasperation.

She looked so woebegone that Wynelle laid aside her Bible and put her arms out with a look of compassion.

Thelma gazed at her through her tears for a moment as if unable to believe that there was a refuge waiting for her and then in a burst of sobs she flung herself across the room and buried her head in Wynelle's lap.

The older girl let her cry it out for several minutes while she smoothed her hair lovingly. Thelma had pretty hair. Just to be different, she wore it pulled back and hanging, with a ribbon around her head, somewhat in the style of Alice in Wonderland. But her hair was glossy and wavy and except when she had her ridiculous big goggles on, she was almost attractive. Only her expression was a little sour, and showed that she spent a good deal of time pitying herself.

Wynelle found herself praying in her heart that she might be given the wisdom to know what to say to this poor little neglected soul.

At last Thelma looked up, her eyes bleary, a desperate question in them.

"Why?" she blubbered.

"Why what, honey?" Wynelle asked gently.

"Why are you like you are? And why are we like we are? I think my family is perfectly horrid. I *hate* every one of them, and I'm sure they hate me!" She put her head down again in a fresh outburst.

Wynelle waited until she was quiet again and then she said, "I think I know how you feel, but I'm sure your family doesn't hate you. I believe I know what your trouble is, although I have only so lately learned the way out myself that I'm not sure I can make it plain to you."

Thelma raised her head with an incredulous look in her eyes while Wynelle went on.

"I used to have spells of feeling very sorry for myself, and it made me quite miserable; partly, I think, because I knew I wasn't worth it!"

Wynelle chuckled a little, as if the joke was on herself. "The whole trouble was that I was all taken up with myself! And it was only when I discovered that Jesus died to get rid of that old 'self' and to give me *Him*self, that I got free."

Thelma put a scornful look on her face, but Wynelle went right on explaining in a loving tone.

"You see, kid," she said, "the Bible makes it very plain that we are all sinners." Thelma made a little sound between a sneer and a snort of contempt.

"Yes, I know what you're thinking," agreed Wynelle, "I heard all the same stuff in school that you did. That we should 'express ourselves,' and that sin is only a comparative term anyway, that our behavior is only 'anti-social.' But we all know perfectly well if we are honest that it's downright selfish and sinful. The Bible says that just 'turning each one to our own way' is sin, because it's not God's way. And all that any one of us deserves is eternal punishment."

Again she saw the look of utter contempt appear as if by force of habit, in Thelma's face.

"But listen," went on Wynelle. "While God is just and has to punish sin, He is also loving, and He has made a way to save us. He sent His own Son down here to be punished in our place! *I* think that's wonderful. In all my life I never realized, when Christmas would come around and we'd sing carols about His coming and all that—I never realized *why* He came. Now that I know I just can't get over how wonderful it is that He should care to do it and suffer all that on the Cross for us, when we were such silly fools in going our own way. As a matter of fact, if you come right down to it, we were actual enemies of God, because I know myself that most of the time when I have been conscious that there was something that I ought to do, I didn't want one bit to do it! It just goes to show how our 'self' is directly contrary to God's will. And that is why it is so wonderful to know that 'God so *loved* the world that He gave His only begotten Son, that whosoever believeth in Him should not perish but have everlasting life!' Now don't *you* think that's wonderful?"

Thelma had forgotten to look supercilious for a few minutes, but when Wynelle appealed to her now she tried to take refuge in her old manner.

"Oh, that old stuff!" she scoffed. "I know they used to talk about sin back in the dark ages. It's just a form of parapraxis. Psychology is our only hope. You know, I believe that some day the psychon will be segregated by surgery! Don't you think so?" Thelma put her chin up and tried to look wise but Wynelle ignored the look.

"That's beside the point," she said. "After all, it was God who created the psychon if there is such a thing."

"Rot!" said Thelma. "I had a Sunday School teacher once who harped on the Bible. You don't really believe all that, do you?"

"Yes, I really do," said Wynelle, "because I've tried it out and I've found that it works. If you really want to know *how* I know, I'll tell you. When I came here, and especially after I hurt my ankle, I never wanted anything so much as to get away. I confess I didn't feel welcome, and yet I didn't see how I could do anything about getting away. In myself I could never have been half decent to any of you, for I felt that I wasn't wanted."

Thelma gave Wynelle a quizzical, disconcerted look.

"I guess we have been pretty mean to you," she admitted, dropping her eyes before Wynelle's gaze. "I told mom yesterday that she ought to feed you more."

"Oh, I have enough, and besides, that's all right now," said Wynelle with a smile.

Thelma stared in amazement.

"Don't you see," explained Wynelle, "I just reckoned that *I* was dead to it all, just like the Bible says to do, and that it wasn't I who was here at all, it was Jesus. I asked Him for all His gentleness and love and somehow, I can't explain it, He gave it to me. I *really* love you."

As Thelma continued to stare, Wynelle drew her teary distorted face to her and kissed her on the forehead.

Thelma did not say anything but her face twisted and again two tears rolled down her cheeks. She looked like a naughty, contrite little child.

"I love you," went on Wynelle, "because God loves you. He loves you *very* much. And I guess, maybe, He sent me here to tell you so, as well as for me to learn a lot myself, which I needed badly to do."

"If He loves me," whimpered Thelma, "why did He put me here where I hate everybody and everything?"

"Let me ask you this, honey," said Wynelle. "Have you ever tried letting Jesus come into your heart?"

"Gosh no! I wouldn't know how. Anyway He wouldn't like it in my heart. I guess it's a mess. I don't suppose I've ever had a really good thought about anybody all my life. I *hate* people. I've hated boys because they didn't pay any attention to me except to make fun of me, and I've hated girls because the boys liked them and not me. There, now," her voice choked, "that's what I really am, I guess. You can see a God wouldn't want me!"

"I don't think you're very different from anybody else. We are all that way naturally, in one way or another. But God says He 'loves' knowing just what we are, and how helpless we are to do anything about it."

"I've tried sometimes," said Thelma meekly through her tears. "You wouldn't think it but I have. Especially since you've been here."

"I don't doubt it," agreed Wynelle. "But you didn't make it, did you?—any better than I or anyone else ever did, of ourselves. Only He can do it. But He can. It works!"

"I don't see how."

"I can't explain *how*, but I know it does!" said Wynelle. "When you come to the place where you are willing to admit that you are just no good, and that you really have sinned, then get down on your knees and tell Him so, and tell Him you are glad that Jesus came down here to take all your sins away. When you have it out with Him like that He will come into you and give you a new life inside, literally. You will find yourself wanting and liking entirely different things from what you did. It's wonderful. I wish you'd try it."

Thelma sat a long time staring off at space. At last she rose to her feet and looked shamefacedly down at Wynelle.

"Well," she said, "I might, some time."

Wynelle smiled with a happy light in her eyes.

"Don't put it off," she warned. "Let Him start right now to make you a new person. I'll be prayin' for you, dear."

Thelma left the room without thanks but Wynelle felt strangely glad. For the first time she could believe that there was some real good in her being in this house.

As she got into bed her eyes sought the little motto that Roger had given her. "Beloved, think it not strange . . . rejoice." To think that in this short time she had learned something of what that really meant.

She lay down to sleep with a prayer in her heart for the young man who had been the means of bringing such peace and joy into her life, wishing he were home, wondering how many days he would be gone. There had been something about the way he spoke of his errand that seemed to suggest that it was serious. Could it be that it had anything to do with his father's status? He had told her very little about his father, but she gathered that the tragedy was never very far from his mind. She wished that she might be of some help to him some time, as he had been to her. She fell asleep hearing the words over and over, "Beloved, beloved, think it not strange. Think it not strange, beloved."

But at three o'clock in the morning she was awakened by someone pulling and shaking her, someone who was gasping in terror.

CHAPTER 15

AT FIRST WYNELLE thought Mona must be having a nightmare. But she reached out in the bed and Mona was not there. Then she switched on the bed lamp and saw that Mona had not yet returned from the Saturday night dance. If she had been the room would have been cluttered with her finery, her shoes on the bed, and her dress in a heap over the footboard. It was not Mona who was pulling at her, it was Della who was crying and shaking her awake, Della in a torn evening gown, her face streaked with tears and smeared with makeup.

"Sh!" warned Della tensely. "Don't let the folks upstairs hear! Wyn, I'm in a terrible jam. I'm terrified to go to dad or mom. But I can't go to bed, I'm too scared. I had to talk to somebody, and there was nobody but you. You'll have to listen to me, and if you tell, I'll—I'll kill myself! Swear you won't tell!"

Horrified, Wynelle sat up in bed and tried to shake the sleep from her.

"What's the matter, Della?" she asked, trying to speak calmly.

"Promise you won't tell!" Della whispered hoarsely.

"I never promise things until I know what they are, but I'll try to help you as much as I can."

"Well, I guess it'll all be out anyway by tomorrow," sobbed the girl. "Oh-h-h! It's an awful mess! Why should *I* have to be the one that was in on it! I didn't do anything so terrible myself, I swear I didn't. Nothing more than I've done lots of other times. Nothing more than all the kids do. But the way the whole thing ended up, I suppose I'll have to appear in court and dad'll just about *kill* me even if they don't send me to the electric chair for murder. Oh-h, I wish I *was* dead!"

Wynelle took hold of the girl's arm and spoke with authority. "Tell me what has happened, Della. Stop your crying and talk to me. I can't help if you don't explain."

Della mopped her face with Mona's end of the sheet and tried to talk.

"It was this way," she started, almost breaking out in sobs again at the horrid memory. "Ted and I were double dating with Nancy Gilkie and Fenton Gilmore—he's a senior from the University and perfectly gorgeous. We had been at the dance at the country club until one o'clock, and the boys had both had too much to drink. They got kind of gay and suggested we go to Washington and see some of the really good night clubs; Fenny has loads of money. So we started out and somebody suggested that we change couples, just for fun. Fenny was driving and I was in front with him. He wasn't too keen about the change, I could tell, because when he put his arm around me he didn't act as if he really liked it. And he kept turning around to see what was going on in the back seat because he's crazy about Nancy. But Ted has always wanted Nancy, and only took up with me because she threw him over a while ago."

Della kept snuffling while she talked. Now and then she would bury her face in the bed covers and shake with sobs. Wynelle felt infinitely older than Della. The sordid story disgusted her, but she waited silently for Della to finish.

"Well, I could tell that Fenny didn't like the way Ted and Nancy were carrying on. I guess Nancy had had too much to drink too, or else she was trying to make Fenny jealous. All at once Fenny gave a kind of an ugly growl and reached back with one arm, to grab Ted, I guess." Della's voice was still tense, a ghastly whisper now.

"But we were going pretty fast and the car headed right for a tree. I grabbed the wheel but I turned it too quick and we skidded and turned over."

Della collapsed in sobs again and Wynelle's heart ached for her.

At last she persuaded her to finish the story.

"Ted and Fenny got out of the car and started to swear at each other and fight. I was so frightened I didn't know whether I was hurt or not. I guess I wasn't. Anyway, I tried to see how bad Nancy was hurt. I couldn't get her to speak. I was scared crazy then. I thought she was dead. It gave me the creeps to touch her. I screamed at the boys and tried to get them to do something but they didn't seem to know what to do. Somebody must have called the police for in a minute they came and took Nancy to the hospital in an ambulance. They made Ted and me go with them to the police station. It was awful, and Ted wasn't any help at all, he was so drunk and so scared. I don't know what became of Fenny. He had disappeared by the time the cops came. They took our names and asked a lot of questions but they didn't seem to believe what I said, because they were terribly cross with me. Oh, do you suppose I'll have to go to court? Or maybe to *jail?* What will they do to me if Nancy *dies?* Oh-h! What'll I do?"

Wynelle hadn't the slightest idea what to do either, but she realized that the problem was far too serious to be taken lightly. She lay a few moments while Della shook and moaned. Then she said, "Della, before I tell you what you have to do, I'm going to tell you something else. It's the *only* thing that can take you through this mess without your going practically crazy. Sit up and look at me. I'm going to tell you straight without any frills. This isn't the time for frills. Now get this.

"You and I and everybody else that ever lived is a sinner. There are plain and fancy sins, but we are all sinners." Della made no attempt to disagree with her.

"God never offered but one way for sinners to be saved, and that is through confessing your sin to Him and accepting His Son as your Saviour. That is the only way to escape *everlasting* punishment. Now what God will decide to do about you here and now I don't know. A lot will depend, I guess, on whether you are His child or not."

Della looked at Wynelle with horrified eyes. She had been afraid of earthly justice, but to have to reckon with a higher court had not entered her mind.

She flared up.

"I didn't come in here for you to preach to me," she hissed, tossing her head.

"Goodness knows I don't want to either!" retorted Wynelle. "But somebody's got to. You know you had no business with a crowd like that, or carrying on like that. You should know that you'd be sure to get into trouble, even if you don't care about doing right for any other reason. If you want me to help you I'll help as well as I can, but you've got to do what I tell you. You're the one who is in a jam, aren't you?"

"Yes," admitted Della tearfully, "but I didn't do anything myself. I don't see why you have to jump on *me*. I don't see anything wrong with petting. Everybody does that."

"You don't see anything wrong with it?" exclaimed Wynelle. "After *this*? Isn't that what got Fenny into this mess? And Nancy, and all of you? I admit it was liquor besides, but then that was wrong too." She tried to calm herself and speak gently. "Listen, Della," she said, "did your mother *teach* you to drink and pet, in order to do right?"

Della shrugged. "Of course not," she answered sullenly.

"Well, why didn't she, if it's the thing to do?"

Della was silent a moment, then she burst out suddenly,

"Oh, I *know* it's not right, Wyn. Lay off the preaching. I admit it."

Wynelle spoke more gently.

"I really don't mean to preach, Della. I know very well if I hadn't started out with a different background I would probably have done the same as you. And we've all sinned in one way or another. Some sins *look* worse, that's all. Some get us into trouble here and some don't, but they all will when we're done with this life unless you take Jesus as your Saviour. You may get into a peck of trouble for this anyway, but why don't you get down on your knees now and tell Him you're sorry and want to be His child. That makes all the difference."

"What would He want with me if I'm so bad?" she whimpered.

"We're *all* bad in one way or another. He says He loves us and wants us saved. You have to believe Him."

Della stood up, irresolute.

"It seems like kid stuff." She started to sneer. "I haven't been down on my knees to say my prayers since I was a tiny little thing."

"And you haven't lived very right since then, either, have you?"

"I suppose I haven't," admitted Della.

"And you haven't been happy?"

"Heavens, *no!*"

"Well, then?"

All of a sudden Della crumpled and buried her head on the edge of the disordered bed, sobbing out her sin and distress.

"Oh God, I guess I've been terrible, but if You can get me out of this, won't You do it? Amen."

Wynelle was not sure whether that prayer would be acceptable to God or not, but it was a start at least. So when Della arose and tried to straighten herself up Wynelle said, "Now the next thing is to tell your father!"

"Oh-h-h!" cried Della under her breath. "I *can't*. He'd kill me. He told me I was never to go with Ted again, nor to drink before I was twenty-one."

"No, he won't kill you. Anyway, you'd be better off dead with this thing confessed, than have it to hide. Would you rather go and tell him alone or do you want me to go with you?"

"You go along," pleaded Della.

"All right, but you're to tell him everything!" she commanded.

With no relish for her task Wynelle dragged herself out of bed and hobbled across to get her housecoat.

Just then the front door opened cautiously and Mona entered.

She started in fright as she saw Wynelle and Della in the hallway.

"What's the matter?" she clutched Wynelle.

"Never mind, you get to bed now, Mona," Wynelle said in a tone of authority.

"Bed! Does that sound good to me! I'm simply pooped!"

Wynelle caught the heavy odor of liquor on Mona's breath also, and she suddenly felt as if she had more responsibility than she could carry.

As she painfully climbed the stairs she felt like sinking down and never rising again. Then out of the darkness she seemed to hear, "Beloved, think it not strange, think it not strange . . . rejoice."

And as if she had had a cool reviving drink she went on to face what was in store in the Snellers' room.

CHAPTER 16

WHEN WYNELLE AND Della reached the door of the Snellers' room Della nearly collapsed.

"I can't do it! I can't!" she faltered in frenzy.

"Do you want the police to come and tell him?"

"Oh *no!*" Della clung to her.

"Then it's the only way," insisted Wynelle firmly.

She knocked lightly on the door. There was no answer and she knocked again.

"Dad has a fit if he's disturbed at night," urged Della. "Let's wait until morning."

"You won't be able to sleep and neither will I. We might as well get it over with." Once more she knocked and this time Alberta's sleep-drugged voice called irritably, "Who is it? What do you want?"

"It's Della," answered Wynelle in a low voice. "She's in some trouble and she needs to talk to her father."

A light showed at the crack of the door and a murmur of voices sounded within. Dick's was impatient but Alberta's was insistent.

Finally Dick appeared at the door in his dressing gown. "What the hell do you want at this hour?" he demanded crossly.

Della dissolved in tears but Wynelle said,

"Della is in a jam and I think you ought to know about it right now. Will you come downstairs and let her tell you?"

"Jam? What kind of a jam?" He took hold of Della's shaking shoulder and demanded, "Speak out! Don't stand there like a nit-wit. What have you done?"

"Oh, I didn't mean to, dad. I didn't really do anything."

"Well, what are you here for then? Why do I have to be waked up at this ungodly hour? For goodness' sake, haven't I trouble enough in the daytime without being pestered at night, too? What's wrong? Make it snappy!" He was fairly roaring now and Wynelle expected that Richard and all the rest, if not the neighbors too, would rouse and rally to the scene.

"We had an accident," Della blubbered. "And—"

"Were you hurt? You seem to be able to get about!" her father said sarcastically.

"No, but I think maybe Nancy was killed."

"Good heavens! Well, what do you want me to do about it now? Was it your fault?"

"No, not exactly. That is, I'm afraid maybe it was. I turned the car and—" Della gave in once more to her tears.

Dick turned to Wynelle.

"Can *you* tell me what happened, or is everybody muddled?"

Wynelle told Della's story in a few words, omitting nothing that seemed of importance to her, even emphasizing the fact that all the young people were drunk.

"Hunh! Crazy young ones! Didn't I *tell* you, Della, that you weren't to go with that rascal Ted? You don't date for a month now! And *never* with him again. I'll see what I can do to fix the judge in the morning. Now for heaven's sake get out and let me get some sleep." He went into his room and slammed the door.

Wynelle, thoroughly shocked at Cousin Dick's lack of concern, followed Della slowly into her room.

Della's tears had stopped and her face was considerably brighter.

"You were right, Wyn, I'm glad it's over with. Oh, what a relief! I'd never have had the nerve to tell him if you hadn't made me. I guess he can fix things all right, don't you? I'd just die if I had to be questioned in court."

Wynelle did not answer right away. It had never occurred to her that anybody could take a calamity like this so lightly.

"Della, listen," she said at last. "You had better begin to be honest with yourself. If all you want is to skin through life the easiest way without getting caught and punished for your sins, don't think you're going to get away with that with God. If I were you I'd get down on my knees after I'm gone and really have it out with Him. Tell Him *everything* that's wrong with you. If you let Him He'll show you plenty that you never realized before. It's the only way to start with a clean slate. You'll feel better. And then you can trust Him with what may happen in court or anywhere else. There isn't *any* other way to have peace in your heart."

"Oh, I feel lots better already," replied Della airily. "You were swell to go with me. Dad'll straighten things up. He'll rave a little at me, but he won't let them put me through the third degree. I know him, he won't want his own name to be mixed up in it. He'll hush-hush the whole thing now."

"But Della! That's not the way to go on through life. You are just avoiding the issue. Didn't you mean what you said downstairs when you got down on your knees?"

"Oh, I don't know. You said I had to do it, and I did it. That ought to satisfy you. Maybe some time when I get old and staid like you I'll get religious too, but that sort of thing doesn't appeal to me now. Besides, I didn't do anything so terrible. Golly, I'm tired. It's been an awful night. Let's get to sleep! Thanks for your help. 'Night."

With a heavy heart Wynelle went out and closed the door, easing herself down the stairs by the railing.

"What is the use?" she thought. And again it came to her to wonder why on earth these matters seemed to be dumped into her lap all of a sudden. Was life to be just one crisis after another now for her? Then as her hand reached in the dark for the newel post, she had a vague subconscious sense that there was something sweet and pleasant connected with that newel post. What could it be? She paused a moment, and then it came to her. On the way upstairs as she had reached for the post to steady her lame foot, there had come that encouraging word to her that had given her the strength to go on and do what she felt she should do, with peace in her heart. She said the words over and over again and they breathed into her soul the same calm and strength that they had before: "Beloved, think it not strange . . . rejoice!" She took a deep breath and smiled. She could almost see the brave strong face that had looked into hers that day on the plane, the smile that seemed to have been born in heaven. Oh, how she longed to see Roger again. Perhaps he could tell her what to do next. The way seemed so bewildering.

Wynelle did not try to go to bed again. She knew from experience that Mona would probably be sprawled all over it anyway, and there were only a couple of hours before she would be getting up now. She might as well just lie down on the couch in the living room.

She threw the tightly stuffed sofa pillows on the floor and pillowed her head on her arm as she turned the whole thing over in her mind, wondering how a girl could possibly want to slide through life the way Della was doing. Would Thelma's apparent change of heart turn out to be as shallow? She sighed in discouragement. The way was so rugged, and in spite of her attempts to sow the right kind of seeds, it seemed as if nothing but thorns and weeds came up.

She lay a long time thinking, until all at once she became aware of the sound of an engine stopping in front of the house. It was probably the milkman. No, this was Sunday. The milkman did not come today. Perhaps the paper boy. But she knew that the paper boy was usually later than this on Sundays, for Dick had often fretted and fumed because it had not arrived when he got up.

Then she heard soft footfalls passing the living room and going on to the window of the room she shared with Mona.

Her heart gave a leap. Could it be that Roger was home again? She sat up and drew aside the curtain. The window over the couch was open and she could see a tall lean figure going past on the way back to the jalopy.

"Roger!" she spoke in a stage whisper.

Like a flash the figure whirled and stopped as if listening.

"Roger! Here! At the front window," she called softly.

With long eager steps he strode to the window.

"Oh, I say!" he exclaimed under his breath. "It's good to know you're better! Can't you come out with me now for that ride?"

There was an undertone of such eagerness in his voice that Wynelle's heart did another leap for joy.

She hesitated a moment. The dawn was just breaking in the east.

"I don't know why not," she said. "Nobody will be up for hours and they won't miss me. I'll get dressed and be out in two jerks."

"Okay," he agreed enthusiastically. "I'll slip back and get my note and meet you out here. Can you walk all right?"

"Yes, I do pretty well," she responded. She was almost ashamed of the joy that surged up in her. She was afraid that he would notice her eagerness in every word that she said. It was *so* good to know that he was home again, and that she was going to have a little time with him!

She limped as fast as she could back to the bedroom and slid into her clothes, just whatever she could lay hands on without disturbing Mona. She reached down under the bed and pulled Roger's sweater out from the suitcase where she had stowed it carefully. The morning chill was in the air and it would feel good. Then she would return it to Roger before they got home.

In less than five minutes she was stealing out the front door where Roger met her and helped her to the car.

In the driver's seat he paused before starting the car and turned to her in the dim light of dawn.

"This is good!" he said and smiled. His words seemed to say so much more than three words generally did. Wynelle smiled back at him, starry-eyed. "It's good to be out again," she replied.

She wanted to add "with you" but she didn't. Then lest he see her soul in her eyes she looked away, her heart pounding.

"We've waited a long time for this ride, haven't we?" he said joyously.

It sounded so cosy and comradely, that "we," thought Wynelle. He was taking it for granted that she was as eager as he for the ride. And she liked that. It showed that he knew exactly how she felt about it; he seemed to know how she felt about almost everything. That was good, good like food and shelter and friends. She snuggled deep into the worn seat and hugged her knees.

He glanced down at the sweater. His eyes told her she looked cute in it.

"Have you had that on ever since I saw you last?" he teased.

She giggled.

"Well, not quite. But it certainly did feel good that night. I don't know what was the matter with me that I shook so."

"That always comes as a reaction when you're hurt. The doctor says you had a pretty bad sprain. I'm glad you're better. Have you had a tough time?"

She looked up at him with desperation. "And how I've had a tough time! That is," she corrected herself, "some things have been tough, but between you and God they've been made really wonderful."

"I'm glad of that." He said it as if it meant a great deal to him.

"You are back before you expected to be, aren't you?" she asked. "I was not looking for you so soon."

He looked sober.

"Yes," he said. "Things worked out much quicker than I had expected." He hesitated as if he considered telling her what was in his mind and then he abruptly changed the subject. "Where do you think you'd like to go, anywhere in particular?"

"No, except that I'd like to see my house again. I've tried so many times to picture it. I thought I remembered every single thing about it from that one visit, but I want to make sure. I just loved it."

Roger looked troubled.

"It seems all wrong for me to be there in your house, when you would like to live there yourself."

"But I'm *glad* you are there!" cried Wynelle. "You know I couldn't go there now, and I don't suppose it would be the thing for me to go there and live all alone at any time. I have been so thankful that it was you, and that I knew you were loving it and taking care of it. I was thinking how nice it would be if you would be willing to stay on at least for a while and take care of it for me. Later perhaps I can find someone to stay there with me. My mother might like to come east and be with me, but I rather doubt it. If I stay here in Maple Grove I will find some nice business woman before long who would rent a room perhaps."

"I would be more pleased than I can tell you to stay there," said Roger, "and I will try to be a good tenant!" He spoke submissively with a twinkle in his eye. "I wouldn't be able to pay what rent the house should bring alone, but if you would be willing for my father to come there and live with me when he is released, provided I can get him a job, the two of us ought to make it together. The old house was sold, you know, and torn down."

"Oh, I think that would be fine. I would love to meet your father some time," she said shyly.

Roger turned and looked squarely at her, slowing the car as he did so.

"Are you sure you would?" he asked challengingly.

Wynelle caught her breath a little. She had never heard any details of the tragedy that had taken place so many years ago. Perhaps there was more than she knew. But whatever the man was, he was Roger's father, and Roger was evidently standing by him. She decided that if he could feel that way about his father she could too.

"Yes," she said earnestly, "I'm sure I would."

He gave her a look of deep gratitude.

"Is he," she asked hesitantly, "is he anything like you?"

Roger did not answer right away and she added, "Or are you like your mother?"

At that Roger winced, and she was sorry she had spoken.

"I—don't know," he said gravely. "I was going to say, 'I hope not' but that might not be fair. I don't remember my mother very well, as she was then."

Wynelle wondered over that.

"As she was then? What—do you mean?"

Roger was silent a long time, thinking, hesitating as if about to talk, and then he closed his lips, after mumbling, "Nothing, I guess."

Wynelle was inclined to change the subject and she cast about in her mind for something else to talk about but Roger took it up again.

"My father will be out this month," he said, but not as if it were a joyous prospect. "You know they shortened his term from twenty to fifteen years." There was a heavy burden of responsibility shadowing his face. He looked haggard, years older than when she had first met him. What a wonderful son, she thought, to care about a father who had brought disgrace on him and made his life a misery.

"I am trying to find somebody who will give him work. It will mean everything if he has something to do right away. Jobs are not too plentiful for anyone, and of course nobody wants a man with his record. Oh, people are polite enough to me about it, at least most of them are, but I can tell that they shy away from having anything to do with him. I don't blame them, I would myself, I suppose, if I were in their position."

Wynelle looked up at him and wondered at the gladness in her heart over this young man, the son of a murderer, or so everyone said, a man who was not allowed in her own cousin's house. Yet she felt that she could trust him beyond anyone she had ever

known. She admired the long clean line of his jaw, the firm set
of his lips, the lines around his eyes that seemed to suggest compassion and sympathy. She knew that he would not be called a
handsome man, yet she loved the way his hair grew around his
temples, the clear look of his sun-tanned skin. She dropped her
eyes to his hands and noted the strength of them, the sure way
he held the wheel. She remembered how those hands had held
her, that day in the plane, and joy swelled up in her to think
that she had had the good fortune to be counted a friend of this
man. She said nothing, but her thoughts were in her face, and all
of a sudden Roger glanced down at her, caught her look and
smiled with that smile like the light of heaven. Their eyes met
and a thrill that seemed to turn her world upside down surged
through her. Her breath came quickly and she turned her head
to hide her feelings. When she cast another glance out of the
tail of her eye at Roger's hand on the wheel she saw that he was
gripping it until the white showed at his knuckles but he said
nothing.

"Here's your house," he told her in an even tone. "Does it look
as good as it did when you first saw it?"

She leaned forward in delight and let her eyes sweep up the
long green lawn, immaculately trimmed, down the other side to
the little stream, and up again, to the quaint line of the brown roof
drenched now in early morning light. Sparkles of dew were on the
lawn and the shrubbery, even on the little pink roses that wan-
dered over the tiny front porch. A little dream place, it was, and
her face lit up with pleasure.

"I can't believe it's mine!" she cried.

Roger smiled at her delight and then he said, "If you're satisfied
to let my father and me stay there a while I'm going to make it
my business to find somebody who will be suitable to be there
with you, when you are ready to make the change."

He spoke as if he were taking a vow. Wynelle wondered at him
again. He did not live carelessly as most young people did. It

seemed as if everything he did had a purpose, and he did it because it was the right and only thing to be done next. It gave him an air of authority, an almost royal bearing. Yet he was perhaps the most humble person she had ever known. She treasured each moment she spent with him and dreaded to have this little time over.

"Want to go in?" he asked her.

She smiled wistfully and shook her head.

"Not this time, I guess. I suppose I ought to be getting back. What time is it?"

He glanced at his wrist.

"Still only seven o'clock." He grinned. "There will scarcely be a soul up in the whole town at this hour on Sunday morning. Unless it's old Mamie Pike. She never goes to sleep, they say, and I almost believe it. She never misses a thing that goes on in the town. I'd ask you in to breakfast if it weren't for her, but she'd talk and I don't want that for your sake. She lives over there across the way. How would it be if we go down to the coffee shop by the railroad station? That's open early and it's really pretty good. That is, if you don't mind appearing in the town with me. I'm a marked character, you know."

Wynelle looked up at him quickly. He was not joking. He spoke gravely and watched her to see how she reacted.

She looked away trying to find words to express what she thought. Then she looked up at him again her big brown eyes gazing straight into his gray ones.

"Roger Blackstone," she said solemnly, using his full name purposely as if to show him that she was not ashamed of that name even though it was his father's, "there isn't a man I ever knew whom I would rather call my friend!"

For a long moment Roger held her gaze, gravely, searchingly, as if he would make sure she understood what she was saying. Then he broke into that wonderful smile again as he laid his hand over hers and gave it a warm grateful pressure.

"I sincerely hope," he said earnestly, "that I shall never give you cause to take that back!"

Wynelle looked trustingly up at him.

"I can't imagine that you would," she said.

"Let's go," he grinned just like a boy again. "I'm hungry."

CHAPTER 17

THERE WAS SCARCELY anyone in the coffee shop. They took a secluded booth at the far end of the room and never realized how the glow of their faces seemed to light up the dreary little room till the tired waitress looked over at them wistfully. She saw so many couples come in there who were half drunk and quarreling, it was refreshing to see two who were wholesome and bright and happy looking.

After they had given their order Roger settled down with content.

"You said things had been tough. Anything special?" he asked with concern. "Your cousin hasn't been trying again to make you sell your house, has he?"

Wynelle shook her head. "No, he's only mentioned it once. He came in one day and said that as I was crippled up and no telling when I'd be able to earn anything and pay my way, I would do well to sell the house right away and have something to go on." She gave a wry smile.

Roger frowned.

"What did you tell him?"

"I said that I still did not want to sell, and that I would pay my board while I was there. But he as much as told me that they had been expecting to have to put up with me for a month anyway, and that I didn't need to begin to pay until after that!"

"The heel!" exclaimed Roger hotly. "Excuse me, I know they are your cousins, but it makes me boil on your account."

Wynelle smiled.

"If you hadn't taught me a lot before I was imprisoned there

165

I would have boiled hard, and boiled over, too, many a time. But I think," she spoke shyly, "that I have learned a little, just a little, about what you meant that day about the Cross. And God has let me serve in a small way too. I don't know that my services will amount to anything in the long run, but I've made a start, and it felt good!" She laughed, and then she told him all about her talks with Thelma and Della.

Roger listened with interest. Now and then his face lit up with that wonderful smile and Wynelle felt as if she had been crowned.

"We'll have to pray for them," he said earnestly. "Della's a tough youngster, always has been. But it sounds to me as if Thelma might really accept the Lord and be transformed. She is young and maybe not too hard, yet, for all her pretended sophistication."

Wynelle suddenly thought of the contrast between this comradely talk with Roger and the dates she had had with other boys. She tried to imagine Bud Hendricks being interested in the spiritual welfare of a stranger-girl of fourteen, or Lammie Odum saying that he would pray with her over anything. That swelling of gladness took possession of her again and she felt as if her very heart were singing.

"It's wonderful what He will do if we let Him, isn't it!" smiled Roger delightedly.

"It sure is!" replied Wynelle. "I wonder what He might have done for me before if I had known enough to let Him? But tell me about your trip. How did you make out?"

The shadow settled heavily over Roger's face and once more he seemed to be years older. He did not answer immediately, then he said,

"It's a long story." He paused and Wynelle thought that perhaps he did not care to tell her anything. Perhaps he felt she had too much curiosity about his affairs. But then he looked straight at her as he said tensely, "I'd like very much to talk it over with someone, but it's not a pretty story."

Wynelle stopped folding and refolding her paper napkin into fantastic patterns, and looked him steadily in the eyes.

"Roger," she said, "I thought you knew me well enough by now to realize that I am not looking for pretty stories. You have helped me in the short time I have known you more than anyone else ever did, and while I don't presume to think that I could help you, if it would do any good for you to have a listening ear, mine is always at your service." She continued to keep her gaze straight on him, never wavering as he looked up to measure her sincerity.

He let his deep gratitude show in the look he gave her, and then said quite simply, "I thank you for that."

But it was some minutes, and the waitress had brought their food and left them again, before he said, "Let's eat breakfast and then go for a ride again and talk, shall we?" She agreed and they chatted about the house and Grandmother Williams while they ate.

When they were out in the car alone together again, he began.

"The first thing I can remember," he said, "was my mother and father quarreling." The suffering that the memories caused him seemed written all over his face and Wynelle's heart went out to him.

"My mother," Wynelle noticed that he never spoke of her as "mother" or "mom," but formally: "my mother." "My mother, as I recall, was almost never home. Dad was always having to take care of me and get the meals when he was home. When he wasn't, I had to make out the best I could. When she would come in she would fly into a rage if he questioned her or asked where she had been. I didn't understand a lot when I was a kid, but some things have come back to me since I have been grown, and I realize that she—that dad"—he stammered as if he hated to state what he had to say, "that he must have been jealous, and I guess with good cause. There was a man named Winters, I remember, who used to come that last year to see her when dad was not home. She said he was a traveling salesman, selling household insurance. Maybe he was. That's one thing I'm checking on now. Anyhow, I remember he was there once when they sent me home from school early and she hadn't expected me. She was very much upset and sent me on an errand."

He broke off to say, "It seems terrible to be talking this way about my own mother. I've never talked this over with anyone before, except once when Gram Williams went over the whole story with me, when I was in law school and decided definitely that I was going to try to reopen the case. She told me some things I had never heard before and they started me off. She was wonderful!" He said it reverently. "I often think, where would I be if it hadn't been for her?"

Wynelle smiled. "I wish I could have known her," she said wistfully. "I always felt as if I had missed something, not being with her."

"You did," he said emphatically. "No mother could have done more for a boy than she did for me."

"I'm glad she did," the girl said softly.

"She thought a lot of you," said Roger bringing his gaze back to the girl beside him. "She treasured every snapshot and every letter from your mother telling what you had said or done. I grew up thinking you must be some prize!"

"Oh!" cried Wynelle with a bashful little laugh. "What a letdown!"

He did not smile.

"No," he said seriously. "I think she knew what she was talking about."

Wynelle hugged her knees, blushing in embarrassment.

"Well, I'm not!" she protested.

"You aren't the judge in this case," he grinned. "Anyway, gram put me onto some things that she had noticed that nobody had brought out at the trial. She worried about not having said anything at the time, but she had not thought much about them, as they did not seem important then. It turns out that they were, at least I think so." He was deep in the tragedy of the case again and Wynelle felt as if he were withdrawn miles away from her. Yet now and again he would turn and give her a grateful look that meant that he appreciated her sympathy.

"The thing that started me off on an actual hunt was—oh, I feel like a heel to be talking over things like this about my own mother and father!" He had drawn up to the side of the road where they could look off at the distant hills, and now suddenly he put his head down on his arms across the wheel and groaned.

Wynelle's heart ached for him. She said nothing, only laid her hand gently, understandingly on his knee to let him know that she realized how hard it was for him. He put his hand over hers and held it close a moment.

After a while he lifted his head and began to talk again.

"Gram was the one who fixed my—fixed the body for burial. She was a keen observer, and she told me that it was then she noticed two things. She said that every time she had ever met my mother she had noticed a red birthmark on her right wrist, but there was none on that body! Of course it had been in the water a long time and that does change things, but when we talked it all over, it still seemed strange. The other thing she noticed was that when she combed the hair it seemed to part naturally on the right side, and she said she could have sworn that my mother always parted hers on the left. But she thought the water could have done that, too. It did not seem to be anything worth mentioning at the time."

Roger was speaking in a low tone, hesitating sometimes from word to word. At times the agony of bringing out the details seemed to be more than he could bear. Wynelle kept her hand in his and held it tightly as if he were a little boy having to go through a difficult trial. Sometimes he would turn his tortured eyes to hers and try to smile.

"I have spent months trying to trace that man Winters and only a short time ago I found he had been killed in a smashup. He was drunk at the time. So there was nothing to be learned from him, I thought. But I did discover that he had married a woman in Seattle named Myra Hibberd. Hibberd was my mother's family name, and the meagre description I could uncover of the woman sounded something like my mother. But according to Seattle records the marriage took place three years before Winters started coming to our house. It must have been when I was about six. And I can't find any proof that my mother was ever in Seattle!

"I have been following other clues and this week end I had a woman in Chicago questioned. She says she was married to Dan Winters in Seattle, and what's more, she admitted having a son named Roger!" He swallowed hard and turned eyes of agony to Wynelle who was suffering over the mystery as much as he was.

"The strangest thing of all," he went on, pausing a moment as if it were hard to speak, "is that the man I hired to do the questioning says that there was a red birthmark on this woman's right wrist!"

They looked at each other in puzzled horror and then with a moan Roger put his head down on the wheel again. Wynelle held his hand close in both of hers and wanted to weep with him. The tangle seemed so hopeless.

"Does your father know?" she asked.

"I can't talk to him about it. He won't let me refer to it. I'll have to eventually, but it only upsets him and I get nowhere."

At last in a choking timid voice Wynelle said, "You are the one who taught me to pray. Can't we pray about it now?"

He raised his head and gave her a long wondering look.

"You're right," he said. "I have prayed about it, of course, but I get bogged down sometimes, just going over and over it in my noodle. It sure would help to have somebody else to pray with."

She bowed her head and said simply,

"Father—" Then she stopped and spoke to Roger. "I read in the Bible that we have the right to call Him that, is that okay? It seems kind of presumptuous."

He smiled gently.

"It sure is okay," he answered radiantly. "Go right on."

"Father," she continued, "we have come to You to ask You to help Roger in this terrible problem he has. Only You know the answer, and You know the right time to tell it. Won't You show him what to do, if he has to do anything. If not, give him peace about it, and You work it out. Please let his father be born again, and take all the bitterness out just as you did for me. Do it for Jesus' sake, Amen."

There were tears in her eyes when she opened them, and there was a light in Roger's face as he looked at her that outshone the morning sun.

He gave her hand a quick strong pressure before he let it go.

"Boy!" he said in a voice deep with feeling. "It sure is *great* to have somebody to pray with. Sometimes I've felt as if I were in this world absolutely alone, except for God. I can't tell how grateful I am that He sent you!" He said the "you" so gently and tenderly that Wynelle could scarcely keep him from seeing how much it meant to her. She cast him a radiant smile and turned away to look again at the hills across the little valley where they were parked.

"How about turning it the other way?" she said. "I can never thank Him enough for sending you to help me."

He smiled again.

"Us got reciprocities, then!" He grinned. The shadow left his face and once more he looked to her just like a boy.

"How about church this morning? Want to go?" he asked as he backed the car and turned it.

"Oh, I'd love it," cried Wynelle. This was turning out to be as delightful a day as yesterday had been difficult. "If you'll stop by the house I can be ready in a few minutes."

"It's still only nine o'clock," he laughed. "Church is not until ten-thirty. I'll drop you off and pick you up a little after ten. Okay? Then maybe we can go to the Glenwood Inn for dinner and—I thought—would you want to go with me to see my father this afternoon?"

"Oh-h!" cried Wynelle softly. "I surely would!"

"It won't exactly be a pleasure excursion," he reminded her.

"I shall love to go," she said with sincerity.

He smiled again. "I've never had anyone else to go with me except gram," he said, "and she wasn't able to go for some time before she died. It will be nice for him to meet somebody new, especially you," he added.

He dropped her at Snellers' where she found everything still quiet. She hobbled around stealthily so as not to disturb them. She had a feeling that if they found she was going with Roger they would surely try to stop her.

She had mended her navy faille suit carefully while she was laid up, and prevailed on Mona, before one of her many shopping excursions, to get her some braid that matched the silk. She had braided a pattern on the good side of the skirt as well as the torn side, so that when the skirt was pressed the tear was scarcely noticeable. She had a fresh white ruffled blouse to put on, but she still had her old shabby blue shoes which she had considered so ruefully before she left Uniontown. There were her white spectator pumps, of course, but she decided that the blue ones looked better with her suit. She had not felt that she should afford any more new ones until she had some money coming in. She smiled now as she thought of how she had wished for new ones "in case she should meet some nice young man." She recalled how she had said to herself that a *really* nice young man would not care whether her shoes were new or not. She wanted to laugh aloud with joy to think that she had been right! There had been a nice young man, and he was *really* nice, so nice that he hadn't cared about her shoes! She went about preparing for church with as much joy in her heart as another girl might have had as she dressed to go to a show or a dinner date.

Apparently no one stirred all the time she was in the house. It seemed a little underhanded to go out and plan to stay out all day without letting anyone know. So, after she had hunted out the vegetables she thought they would be using for dinner, she washed them, peeled the potatoes, and left them in a deep dish of water. Then she wrote a little note saying that she was going to church, and that she had been invited out to dinner, not to wait for her. Signing herself, after a moment's thought to make sure it was sincere, "Lovingly, Wynelle," she went out on the porch to wait for Roger's car.

But for all her caution, it was only a few minutes later that the Sneller household was rudely aroused by the ringing of the doorbell. They were all still sleeping except Thelma who had been lying in bed soaking up a psychological murder mystery. She had breakfasted on a bag of chain store caramels and the sticky papers were lying like dead leaves about the wastebasket that she had pulled up beside her bed.

She had awakened to the memory of her talk with Wynelle the night before, and she decided that perhaps if she could find a Bible she might read a little in it and see whether there was anything in what Wynelle had said. But she didn't know where to find one. She even went downstairs and rooted around in the bookcases, but there was not a Bible to be seen. So she took an apple and went back to bed to her caramels and the story she had started the day before. But for some reason she could not become absorbed in it. All that Wynelle had said kept coming back to her mind.

When the doorbell rang so insistently she decided that it was probably somebody for Della, a boy to get her to play tennis, or perhaps to go swimming. She glanced over at Della in her twin bed. She was only half undressed, and sleeping heavily. Thelma shrugged and didn't bother to waken her. She'd had too much to drink; that was plain. She would waken with a headache and she wouldn't feel like playing, so why bother? She tried to go on with her reading and let the bell ring. Whoever it was would soon give up and go on their way when they found that everybody was still asleep.

But the ringing did not stop. Again and again it broke the Sunday morning stillness, until at last Thelma heard her mother go padding down the stairs in bedroom slippers.

Thelma had not roused to the disturbance the night before when Wynelle and Della had come up to talk to Dick. She had not heard the sound of her parents' voices in distressed altercation for some hours after the two girls had gone back to bed. Now she heard a man's authoritative tones and her mother's worried ones, then her mother coming heavily up the stairs again. She wondered who the caller was. Probably some boy friend of Della's and her mother was coming to waken her and ask if she wanted to go out.

But her mother's steps went into her own room and the door closed. She could hear her father's angry voice in a low rumble. She tried to ignore it for she was not unused to their arguments, but suddenly the door of her parents' room opened and then her own door burst open and her father stalked in and over to Della's bed. He shook Della roughly by the shoulder.

"Get up!" he ordered irritably. "Get some clothes on, and get downstairs as fast as you can. The police are down there. You'll have to answer questions. I don't know why the devil I have to have the kind of children who can't keep out of trouble!" He swore under his breath, giving the torpid Della another vehement shake. She roused at last and tried to sit up, but she fell back, dizzy, putting her hand uncertainly up to her aching head.

At that he gave her a violent pull and yanked her to a sitting position.

"Wake up!" He gave her another shake. "You got yourself into this mess and you'll have to come down and do something about it. Now get a move on!"

He stormed out of the room, reaching vainly for the belt of his bathrobe which was trailing behind him.

Thelma in her monstrous glasses looked like a solemn owl as she sat in her own bed and watched. She recognized her father's tone of voice and knew that this was no ordinary temper he was in. This meant something serious. She would do well to be on hand.

So she dressed hastily and slid down the back stairs to listen while Della crawled into her housecoat and descended the front stairs unsteadily, the tears of fear streaming down her unwashed cheeks and making last night's smeared makeup even less attractive than before.

CHAPTER 18

THE CHURCH SERVICE was simple and informal, in a plain frame building that was clean but not beautiful. The minister was an old man with white hair and a shining face. He was terribly crippled, Wynelle noticed as he was helped down from the platform after the service.

"He's been that way for forty years," explained Roger. "He says he used to ask the Lord to make him well, but that he has begun now to realize that he has learned to know Him a lot better this way than if he had been free to come and go and be busy about his own affairs. I think maybe he's got something there!"

Wynelle studied him again with wonder. When Roger introduced her the old man gave her a smile like a blessing. How marvelous, she thought, to be such a person that everyone who came in contact with you felt blessed. How few old people were like that! It must have cost a great deal in suffering, but she decided that perhaps it was worth it.

"He is almost the only person who asks after my father as if he were a real human being and not a horrible curiosity," Roger told her when they were out in the car again. "In the days when he was able to get about he went out to see him a few times. He explained God's plan of salvation and tried to get him to see God's way of it. But while my father used to go to church and all that, he wasn't ever born again, and this thing made him hard and resentful. He won't let me say a word about the Lord to him, although I tried again after I was in college and understood the gospel better. He is so sure he is good enough. He won't see that all of us are sinners by nature and that's what makes us sin. He thinks that because he didn't commit this crime he is all right."

Wynelle glanced up with an involuntary question in her eyes which Roger did not miss.

"You are wondering whether he really is innocent, of course. I don't blame you," he added. "I would myself. Well, I know that he is, because he was with me the whole time that it would have had to take place. He had been away for a week and he came home early, before my mother expected him. She wasn't there and he took me out fishing. We took a picnic supper and drove several miles. We didn't get back till long after dark. But nobody happened to see us, and of course the word of a little boy, especially the son of the accused, would not stand in court. I used to hate your Cousin Dick because he called me a little lying brat in front of the whole courtroom. I don't blame him now for I suppose that's the way it looked to him. But I wasn't lying and it got me down then. I never forgot it and I used to plan how I could get it back on him until I got to know the Lord."

"I'm afraid I'd have knocked him down if I had been you, that morning in his house when he was so mean to you. I wanted to, myself! When you try to please the Lord it means that you can't ever fight again, doesn't it?"

Wynelle spoke so regretfully that Roger laughed aloud.

"Boy, it sure sounds as if you'd spent your life in barroom brawls. It's going to be hard for you being a Christian, isn't it?" he teased with a wicked twinkle in his eye. "I didn't know I was going around with a female Joe Louis!"

Wynelle joined heartily in his laughter.

"No, really," she chuckled, "I'm serious. There are lots of times when if I were a man I'd like to give somebody a good licking. And I think it would be right, too."

"Okay, Josephine Louis," he teased. "I think so too. All kidding aside," he said soberly, "I agree with you that Christians sometimes get the idea that Christ was a namby-pamby wishy-washy sort of man. He was nothing of the sort. But the whole question has to do with whose rights we are fighting for. If it's our own, we can't fight. Because in the first place, we're sinners in God's sight, all of us, convicted and sentenced; from one end of the Bible to the other that's made plain. What rights has a criminal, I ask you? But if we are fighting for the rights of someone else who needs help, or we are fighting for His rights, that's different. The trouble is, a lot of the time we mistake the person who is making us uncomfortable for our enemy. Our enemy is the devil, not the person who seems to be making the trouble. Get it?"

"I think I do, at least I begin to," said Wynelle thoughtfully. "That helps a lot. I never had any use for unmanly men who wouldn't or couldn't fight and gave as their excuse that they were Christians and so they mustn't."

"I'm with you one hundred percent on that!" agreed Roger, maneuvering the car to a parking place behind a cosy little tea room nestled among trees.

Wynelle was delighted with the charm of the place.

When they were seated Roger studied her a moment and then said,

"You are a lot like your grandmother, do you know it?"

"I'm glad of that," she smiled. "She must have been wonderful."

"She was," he agreed. "I guess she had a pretty tough time with me for a while, though. I was a little demon in school and when I first went to her I must have been hard to manage. I had had my own way a great deal at home because my mother didn't care what I did so long as it didn't bother her, and my father was a traveling salesman, away a great deal. I was grateful to gram right from the start because she was the only one who seemed to care, but I guess I was awfully impudent to her, and I wanted my own way a lot. She used to read to me often by the fire evenings, and tell me stories. She told me a lot about her son who was killed in the war, you know. I grew up idolizing him."

"That must have been my uncle Dave," spoke up Wynelle.

"Well, it may be she painted him in bright colors, but I guess she wasn't far wrong about him. I've since heard from some who knew him in college and in the army that he was a sharp guy, and afraid of nothing. I remember the day she took me out to the garage and showed me a strap hanging there, the one that they used to use on him. I was amazed, for I had always supposed from what she said that he had never done anything wrong. But she explained that most of the stories she had told me were about him when he was pretty well grown, and that he had had to have a lot of whippings when he was young. I looked at that strap a long time and had a great deal of respect for it. Not long after that she was working in her garden one day and she showed me a plant that had sharp thorns an inch or more long on it and little blood red flowers. She told me that was the kind of plant they used to make the crown of thorns for Jesus. She told me how the Bible said that even He who had never sinned, had to learn to obey by the things He suffered. That made a great impression on me, too. It was not long after that that I really took Him as my Saviour and the next time I disobeyed her I felt so terrible that I went out into the garage and brought her the strap. I really wanted her to use it for I knew I deserved it. And *I mean she did!* I could see it nearly killed her to do it, but she went through with it. She was a great little woman."

"Does your father know all this?" asked Wynelle.

"Oh, I don't remember whether I told him or not. He thought a lot of gram, and was grateful to her and all that, but he never would listen when she talked about being saved. He said, 'Saved from what? I haven't done what they say I have, and I don't deserve to be here.' That's all you can ever get out of him. He gives you a buildup about how everybody has to live the best they can—as if anybody ever did!—and that although the world is all wrong, if you take your share of the troubles in it without complaining God will see that you come out all right in the next life. But he knows the way to be saved. If he could only realize once that he is a sinner, he'd be a different person. He goes his own way there in the jail, has very little to do with anybody, and he seems more surly and unfriendly every year. His term was cut from life to twenty years, you know; and then reduced to fifteen. That's why he'll be out this month. And I've just got to find him work." Roger looked troubled again.

"He was a good salesman, but that's out of the question now, for his confidence is all gone. He never had any specialized training when he was young, and in the prison they've had him making shoes. I gather from what he says that he was never very good at it and he has always hated it. Fifteen years of it has probably been enough. I am afraid there will be nothing better than a janitor's job. I can get him that, but it will wipe out what little self-respect he has. Still it can't be helped. I only hope he'll be willing to take that. Every time I've broached the subject he has just turned away from me with a shrug of contempt as if I thought that was all he could do." Roger sighed and shook his head.

"Would you think it better for him to go away to a new place and start again?" asked Wynelle.

"I've suggested that but dad won't hear to it. He is so bent on protesting his innocence that he insists that he must stay here and prove to people that he is not what they think. I think myself it's usually better to stay where you are after a disgrace and battle it out than to run away. But in this case it might be better to go where he is not known. Still, he won't do it. I confess I admire him for it, but it seems like fool's courage."

Wynelle was silent. There seemed to be no way in which she could help. Her heart ached for Roger.

On the way to the penitentiary both of them were silent and thoughtful. It was Wynelle's first visit to a place like that, and she felt apprehensive.

She gave a little involuntary shudder as they entered. Roger noticed it and the shadow crossed his face again.

He hesitated.

"Are you sure you want to come in with me?" he asked with

concern. "You could wait in the car, you know. I won't be long. It isn't fun here, I admit."

She looked him steadily in the eye again.

"Of course I want to come in," she said with a little straightening of her back and a lifting of her chin. "I *want* to meet your father."

Roger gave her a look that seemed to surround her with his thanks like comforting arms, and they went on.

The strange heavy odor of the place struck her like a forbidding personality. It smelled like a combination of unwashed human beings, antiseptic soaps, and damp cement floors, seasoned as it were with deadly despondency.

She tried to suppress another shudder, and Roger drew closer to her as if he were aware that it was not easy for her.

Wynelle had a sudden terrifying inclination to scream and run when the first heavy door swung shut and was locked behind them. It was reassuring to have Roger walking by her side. She was reminded of the Presence of which she had been so gratefully conscious those first difficult days after she had sprained her ankle. How completely she had come to trust this man who was beside her! Yet his father was a criminal! No, his real father was God. That made all the difference. That was what it meant to be born again. Perhaps she would not have felt this sense of perfect confidence in Roger if he were not a Christian. In that case he would have been merely the son of Morton Blackstone, a lifer whose term had been shortened by a relenting judge.

She stole a look at Roger, stalking along beside her. The shadow was deep upon his face now and her heart went out to him. What it must have been for him to tread this place for fifteen years! What a man he must be, not to give in to utter discouragement in all that time! She had a sudden realization of how this suffering had had its part in making him the man he was, and she felt humbled and sobered by the thought. Looking at it that way, one could actually learn to rejoice in trials, as the little motto had reminded her again that morning while she was stepping softly about Mona's room dressing for church.

Many times a day that word flung its bright message to her heart and encouraged her. How wonderful if the men behind these bars could learn it. She found herself praying that the man who was Roger's father according to the flesh might be born again, as she had been.

After traversing several gloomy corridors, they finally reached a small room and were told to wait. There were heavy iron bars across the end of the room and a passageway behind them. In a few moments the guard reappeared with another man in striped clothing. The guard let him into the space behind the bars and closed the door locking him in. Roger rose, not eagerly, and shook hands through the bars with his father.

Wynelle forced herself to stand and walk toward him. It was a shock to realize that this miserable hard-faced, resentful-looking prisoner was actually Roger's father. Somehow she had had the feeling that Roger's father would not look like the rest of the prisoners of whom she had caught glimpses through bars as they passed down the halls. This man's hair was shaved close like the others, his hands were calloused and his eyes looked hopeless just like theirs. The only difference between him and some of the rest was that he was neatly shaven and looked clean. He stared at her without any lighting of his face in welcome. She put out her hand but he was slow to return her handshake. He seemed the epitome of bitter despair.

In spite of Roger's eager introduction, and her own attempt to speak cheerily, their conversation was desultory.

Roger recounted the various attempts he had made to secure work for his father and the look of resentment deepened in the prisoner's face, but he said nothing.

"I guess it'll have to be the janitor's job at the hotel," said Roger reluctantly. His father's face hardened a shade more.

"It doesn't pay much, but it will be something. Then when

people realize that you are taking your place again, maybe something else will turn up." Roger spoke doggedly, as if he had made up his mind to say these things, and they must be said. But there was no spontaneity in his tone. He dragged out an incident or two about the townspeople and spread them before his father, as it were, for him to view, as one would try to interest a small fretful child by pictures in a casual magazine. But there was no more response to them than a fretting child generally gives, and Roger finally gave up. Wynelle, moved by his struggles, attempted to put in a bright remark now and then but it seemed there was nothing to talk about. The man made no effort to be pleasant on his own account.

"All he seems to have in his mind is the injustice of his being there," Roger said in a discouraged tone to Wynelle when at last the guard came for them and they started with relief down the corridors on their way to outer brightness. "I don't blame him, of course, but there must be plenty of things that happen here that he could tell about, just to be pleasant and let me know that he is glad I've come."

"Have you told him about the woman in Chicago?" asked Wynelle.

"No, with him in this mood I'm afraid to bring it all up again until I have something more concrete and have all the proof in hand. I have pumped him all I can for information. He knows I'm trying to work on it but I don't think he has much hope of my accomplishing anything. I'm afraid I don't myself, sometimes. This last development is the most significant thing I've found and I still can't make sense out of it."

Wynelle longed to help him.

"It seems so terrible for you to have a cloud like this over you," she said. "And it won't be easy to have your father at home all the time, I can see that."

"No." Roger gave a sigh like a groan. "I'm not looking for anything easy. I admit I'm not anticipating his coming out. I don't know that I'll be able to handle the situation. It's hard for a man at best to take his place in life again. And in his case, with his attitude, it may be very hard. I'll count on your prayers, if I may." He put her into the car as if she were something very precious and walked slowly and thoughtfully around to take his seat.

As he got in he glanced at her and she looked so distressed that he smiled.

"Don't take my troubles to heart so, Wyn; it will come out all right. I suppose I shouldn't have worried you with it."

She looked reproachfully at him.

"Haven't you discovered yet," she asked wistfully, "that I *want* to be of some help if I can? You have done more for me than I can ever tell you, let alone thank you for."

At that he looked deep into her eyes as if he would walk right into her soul. Then he swallowed hard and tore his gaze away. She did not guess how nearly he yielded to the temptation to take her in his arms and tell her that he loved her. Only the recollection that he was the son of a man in prison for murder held him back. He had had it all out with himself the night before on the plane, and had decided that it would not be fair to her to take that advantage. But he did not know that the look that he gave her thrilled her from head to foot and she almost cried out with the pain and the joy of it.

There was sweet silence between them for a little as they started back to Maple Grove. Roger was thinking what it could mean to have a girl like this one beside him all the time, loyal and loving and brave. He was trying to control the longing to speak, to tell her that he loved her, to take her in his arms. And Wynelle was seeing again that look in his eyes and wondering whether it meant all that she thought it had meant, or whether she was being foolish and imagining something that wasn't there.

In spite of themselves their eyes were drawn to each other again and each of them began to read there what was in the other's heart, when all of a sudden there was a raucous honking behind them, and a grass-green streamlined convertible tore past them edging Roger far over toward the ditch. He swerved to avoid being hit and glared after them.

There were four young people in the car, three on the seat and one, a highly ornamented girl in a strapless dress, sitting on the lap of the boy on the right. As they passed, the boy leaned far over the side of the car and gave a loud guffaw right into their faces, at which they all laughed loudly.

It was Richard Sneller.

Wynelle gave a gasp of astonishment and anger. Her eyes blazed and her fists tightened. She opened her mouth to speak but she was so indignant that she could not utter a word.

Roger looked at her and laughed gently.

"How now, Josephine?" he teased. "Wouldst pound yon rascal?"

Wynelle relaxed into a reluctant laugh but she gave her head a toss in a little independent way, and exclaimed, "I never knew anybody I *despised* like that boy!"

Roger watched her with merriment in his eyes, but Wynelle could scarcely keep back tears of anger and chagrin. She had a feeling that Richard had snatched from her a very precious moment that could never be recovered.

CHAPTER 19

ON MONDAY MORNING Wynelle accompanied Dick to his office with a great deal of trepidation. The thought of working for him day after day seemed even less attractive than it had last week. She could not forget his careless irresponsible attitude in regard to the injury of Nancy Gilkie. She knew that none of the family had even called the Gilkies on the phone to ask about Nancy, for Dick and Alberta had discussed the matter Sunday evening as they ate crackers and cheese at the kitchen table. The Snellers did not have any regular meal Sunday evening as they always slept late in the morning and had a heavy dinner in mid-afternoon. The younger ones had come in and got a snack each for himself at different times, and Wynelle was cleaning up their dishes and crumbs when Dick and Alberta came in hungry. They seemed to pay no more attention to her than if she had not been there.

"I think you ought to call the family," insisted Alberta. "It doesn't look well not to."

"Nonsense!" retorted Dick. "If I do it looks as if I was admitting that Della was in the wrong. I've called the hospital and the girl is still alive. That's enough. They are holding that out-of-town boy pending further investigation. It looked bad for him from the start because he tried to get away. I doubt if they'll even question Della again. It will probably all pass off and be forgotten."

"Unless the girl doesn't live," shuddered Alberta as she spread a thick coating of mayonnaise on her sandwich.

"Oh hell!" Dick turned on her. "Can that pessimistic talk! Haven't we had a bad enough day without you harping on what *might* happen? I have enough worries. There's talk of political

186

investigation. That will raise particular dickens. But I'm glad at least that I don't have that worthless stenographer in the office any more. She has been a pain in the neck. I can count on somebody in the family, I should hope!" He left a significant pause to let that sink thoroughly into Wynelle's consciousness.

On the way down to the office in Dick's car the next morning he gave his young cousin to understand that she would be held responsible for keeping her mouth shut about anything that went on at the office.

"People come with their confidences, you know, and you will hear a lot and take dictation of a lot of letters that have to do with cases. You are never to open your mouth to *anyone* about anything you know. You might even make me lose a case if you did. Do you understand that?"

Wynelle drew herself up with dignity and said quietly, "I should think that would go without saying!"

He only gave a grunt of satisfaction and said no more during the ride to town.

He worked Wynelle harder than she had ever worked in Uniontown but she did her work well and swiftly. She knew that she was a good stenographer and she rather expected some commendation for her first day when they went home in the evening, but he made no reference to it. He seemed to be mulling over some problem in his mind and she let him alone. It was likely that Gilkie situation, which, Wynelle thought, should be quite enough to keep his thoughts busy.

But at dinner all the reference he made to it was, "How is your friend, Della?"

And when she said she was holding her own, he remarked, "Well, I only hope she stays alive until I land that Commonwealth Attorney job. You *would* pull a thing like this just when I needed to have everything go well." Then he subsided into gloomy musing again.

Wynelle did not see Roger for several days. She had a note from

him saying that he might have to be out of town again soon. She
felt very much alone once more. How he had come to fill her
whole thought!

Now that she was able to be about, Richard was begging for a
date again. She had no desire to go with him, but he kept pressing
her so that it became embarrassing to refuse. He pinned her
down so that she had no way out unless she told him flatly before them all that she did not like him. So when he held her
to it to set a date when she *could* go, if she couldn't go soon, she
finally gave in and told him to make it Friday of the next week.
She secretly hoped that something would come up before that
time that would hinder the date. She wondered why his parents
did not try to stop him nagging her so annoyingly, but they paid
little attention. All they seemed to care about was that money
should not be spent unnecessarily. Dick was continually at Alberta and the children about it. She puzzled over that for Dick's
business seemed to be going well as far as she could tell.

On Thursday afternoon a stout well-dressed man whose name
Wynelle recognized as that of a prominent politician came into
the office and demanded to see Dick. She knew Dick was ex-
ceptionally busy preparing for an important case the next day so
that she was quite surprised when Dick told her to show him
in at once. They went into Dick's office and shut the door. She
thought no more about him except to notice that when he went
out he seemed greatly relieved whereas he had looked distressed
when he first came in. On the other hand, it was Dick now who
seemed distressed. She could not help noticing the transformation.
How pleasant it would be, she thought, if Dick would take the
trouble to relieve the burdens of his family as effectively as he did
those of his clients!

The incident passed out of her mind until just before closing
time, when Dick came to her to have some notes revised which
he was to use in court the next day. Without thinking she ex-
pressed her astonishment at their content.

"Why, I thought you were so sure of winning this case against those men from Cuba," she said. "You said they were racketeers of the worst sort!"

Dick blazed at her in fury.

"And *I* thought I had made you understand that what goes on here is none of your business!" he retorted with an oath. "You write what I tell you to write and shut up! If I have found further light on the case, what is that to you?"

His face was red in his indignation and Wynelle closed her mouth. Dick left soon after that and she was glad. But when she went into his office to get the record from the tape recorder for her next day's typing, she discovered that Dick had left the machine turned on. He surely must have been upset! That meant that he would be a bear at home tonight. What a break that she would not have to ride home with him!

That evening at the table Richard put on an important air and asked his father how the matter of the Cuban racketeers was going. Ordinarily the children paid very little attention to their father's cases. It always seemed to Wynelle that they simply took him for granted as if he were a human bank account. But the Cuban case was receiving a good deal of publicity and she supposed that Richard, hearing it discussed perhaps in the hotel where he worked as clerk, thought that he should be at least as well informed about it as the man in the street. Still she was not prepared for the torrent of rage that Dick let loose upon his son.

Dick wanted to know why on earth or places under the earth, should he have to be pestered with business when he got home after having it to battle with all day? And did his family think that he didn't know how to run his own affairs that they had to butt in and ask questions that were none of their business? And didn't he have enough worries already without having them thrown back in his face all the time?

The family, accustomed in some measure to the father's outbursts, immediately became dumb, all but Alberta who tried ineffectually to rally and make small talk so as to pretend that nothing was wrong.

Wynelle was embarrassed. She caught Della making a grimace at Dick under cover of her napkin, but her father did not miss it and turned his invective on her, finally calling her practically a murderer.

At that Alberta intervened, and Dick, exasperated, shoved his chair back with the meal only half eaten and stormed out of the room and upstairs. Those who were left at the table held their peace until they heard his door slam shut and then they began to bicker among themselves, all except Wynelle, and Thelma who considered herself above such childishness unless it directly concerned herself.

Heartsick, Wynelle sent them all out of the kitchen after supper and did the dishes alone, wondering if any of them would ever be willing to let the Lord have His way in their hearts and change them. She felt lonely, more lonely than she had been since she left Uniontown. Roger was still away and she was beginning to realize that nothing seemed the same when he was out of reach.

But the next morning when she started to take off the letters Dick had dictated the day before, she had reason to be more troubled than ever, so much so that she was distressed to know what to do.

The machine had evidently been left on all the time that the stout politician had been there, and before Wynelle was aware, it had reported to her a good deal of their conversation.

In growing consternation Wynelle heard the visitor's gruff voice say bluntly:

"You want that Commonwealth Attorney job, don't you? You know, I guess, that this mess over the Gilkie girl doesn't help? Well, I can still throw it your way if you will fall into line. Emanuel Sanchez is my biggest account. He is harried to death by this suit that's on. If I can assure him that he will win his case it will mean everything. That's your price. Pay it or else. You said that nobody knows about all that evidence you dug up. Well, lose it! That's all you have to do. Nobody will be the wiser."

Wynelle sat paralyzed with horror. That Dick had done as the politician had suggested she could not doubt. Now she knew why he had changed the notes for his case. It was too late for her to remonstrate. He was already in court this morning. She was glad he was not here, for she would scarcely know what to do if he had found her listening to what had gone on yesterday. Yet she had done it unwittingly. And now what should she do? What she had discovered made her responsible. Or did it? She was so confused that she could scarcely tell what was the right course for her to take. How she wished that she did not know anything about the case at all. If only Roger were at home! But he was in Chicago again and she did not know when he would be back. Besides, she had practically given her word of honor that she would never talk to anyone about what went on in the office.

All the morning her mind was in a whirl. She knew that she had to get the letters out on time, but that conversation kept going over and over in her mind. She wished that she had not left the record on long enough to hear it. Why had she not cut it off as soon as she realized that it was not meant for her? She had been so stunned by what she heard that she had been slow to act. Now she did not know whether to face Dick with it or whether to try to act as if she did not know. Perhaps she ought to seek out someone in authority and tell him the whole thing.

She tried to pray, but her thoughts were in such a tangle that she was afraid that not even God could make anything out of them. She knew that if she faced Dick with what she knew he would fly into a terrible rage and no telling what he would do to try to keep her from making it public. Yet she was aware that if it was right for her to tell she must not flinch from what it would cost her.

All morning long she thrashed it out. At noon she went to

lunch in the little cheap restaurant nearby. While she waited for her sandwich and coffee she put her aching head down in her hands and cried in her heart:

"Oh Lord, if I should do anything, You show me. I'm not sure what is right, whether to go back on my word, or to make this thing known. I'm going to count on You to *make* me do the right thing, or else You do something about this. I'm willing to do anything You want no matter how hard it is."

With a measure of peace she ate her lunch, wishing again that Roger were home, although she was not sure that it would be right to tell even Roger. Very likely Dick would be more angry to have Roger know this than anyone else.

When she went back to the office she half hoped that Dick had been in and discovered for himself what had happened. But there was the record beside her desk. She took it up and looked at it as if she wished it had never existed. Then she walked over to where the others were filed and put it away. If she was to do anything with it later, she would, but until she knew what to do she would just leave it where it would ordinarily belong and let it go at that.

Dinner that night was a rather strained affair. The Cuban case figured largely in the papers and Dick's failure to come through with evidence that had already been hinted at produced something of a shock in business and legal as well as political circles. But Dick's family knew enough now not to bring up the question and Wynelle was glad for she was sure that she would not have been able to maintain any degree of indifference about it.

She found herself avoiding Dick's eyes. Yet why should she? It was he, not she who had done the wrong. But she had a feeling that he might discover from her face what she was thinking. Oh, why had she ever consented to work for him? She had never really trusted him. But she had not had any idea that he was actually crooked. It made her feel as if she could not trust anybody at all. Would even Roger turn out to be dishonest after he had been in the world as long as Dick? Was it necessary for a man to compromise with evil in order to gain what the world called success?

She was heavy-hearted when she went to bed that night. She almost wished for the days when she had had to lie and suffer with her foot. She had thought then that she was in a rather impossible position but her situation now was so much worse that she shuddered with the responsibility of it. How she wished that she could count on a note or some message from Roger there under the screen tomorrow morning! What a help those notes had been. Well, God had provided help for her then, why could He not do it now? She knelt beside the bed before she climbed in, and poured out her heart to God. While she was on her knees Mona came in and seeing her there gave a mocking laugh.

"For cat's sake!" she cried impiously, "cut the camp-meeting stuff and come here and help me with this splinter. It's in my right hand and I can't get it out with my left."

With a last plea for patience Wynelle arose and went to help her. And as she did so her eye caught Roger's text that she had hung over the bed on her side of the wall: "Beloved, think it not strange . . . rejoice!"

Rejoice! What cause for rejoicing could there possibly be in all this?

CHAPTER 20

SATURDAY WAS THE end of Wynelle's first week at the office. When she received her check she looked at it with no small degree of interest. Nothing had been said about how much it would be, and since she had discovered Dick's lack of reliability, to put it mildly, she was more than apprehensive about the amount that she might expect.

But when she saw "Three dollars" written on the little piece of paper her heart sank. She didn't know whether to laugh or cry. Her indignation and disappointment seemed to be all tangled up with her reasoning so that she could not think clearly. She did not trust herself to talk to Dick about it. She felt she must get away alone to get her bearings. It was nearly noon and she was glad to tell Dick that she had some errands and would not be going home with him.

She walked over to the little park and sat down for some time staring at the check. She tried to figure out the situation from the Sneller point of view.

They knew as well as she did that the very least she could expect to get a decent room for would be five dollars a week, and she would have to pay a minimum of two dollars a day for board. That made eighty dollars expenses during a four-week month, more in the longer months. But she had hoped that her services would be considered worth twenty-five dollars a week at the least. She had been making more than that in Uniontown. Well, it looked as if her next problem was to find another job and another boarding place. Until then she would have to make the best of it at the Snellers'. It was frightening how fast her second hundred dollars was dwindling. She knew Dick well enough by this time to realize that to raise a question about what she should be paid would be worse than useless, especially in the mood he had been in the last week. There was nothing to do but wait and seek and pray.

But the tears would come to her eyes as she thought over the injustice of her position. If she had not carried her share and often more than her share of the work at the Snellers' there might be some excuse for her to be charged such high board. But she had been so willing to help that more and more the heavy end of the housework was falling to her lot whenever she was at home. And any room she would rent would certainly be more to her taste than the small share she had in Mona's untidy cubbyhole.

At last, half angry with herself, she wiped her eyes and arose to go forth and seek what she could find to better herself. But she spent the whole afternoon and walked weary miles without result. It was out of the question for her to find a room until she was assured of a different job, for she well knew that Dick in his present mood would never pay her what she was worth. He had recognized a good thing in her and would see that he kept it if possible. She finally trudged back to the Snellers', deciding that as soon as Roger got back she would ask him to try to find her something in Middle City. There would surely be more opportunities in a larger town.

The thought of Roger reminded her of his problems and she was ashamed of herself for considering hers. He had much greater difficulties to face than she did. She knew that his father was due to be released on Sunday. That would mean that she would not see as much of Roger herself, for he had told her that he planned to spend all his spare time with his father to try to keep him from feeling desperate. She was ashamed of her selfish thought as soon as it presented itself and she made up her mind that she would try to think up ways to make things easier for Roger.

She hugged the fact that she had a house of her own to offer them. And then instantly another ugly thought stole into her mind. Roger had said nothing more about paying her rent. She had been in Maple Grove a month and he had been living in her house all that time. Was he, too, going to turn out to be so fond of money that her ideal of him would have to crash with everything else? All that the Snellers had said about him returned in full force. She fought the implication by recalling all the good qualities that she knew were in Roger but it still persisted. She went to bed that night with the feeling that everything she had ever known or loved or trusted in had failed her. But the last thing that her eyes lighted on was "Rejoice!" How could she? The tears would come and she fell asleep at last with her pillow wet.

The little restaurant in Chicago had been doing a steady business all day. People were returning to the city for the fall and winter grind. Unending hamburgers and streams of spaghetti poured through the kitchen into the dining room and their remnants found their way later to Myra Foster's sink to be sloshed off and forgotten.

More weary than usual, lonely and utterly discouraged, Myra stood hour after hour, resting her weight first on one hip and then on the other. Sometimes she removed her shoes to ease the insistent aching in her feet. The day had been dreary outside again. Relentless wind and rain lashed at the building so that they had to keep the one small window in the kitchen closed. That made the air so stuffy that Myra thought she would faint. The cheesy smell on the spaghetti sickened her. She could not eat anything herself. She dreaded the hours she had yet to work. But she dreaded worse the time when she would have to start back to her cold dismal room in the rain.

Lately thoughts had haunted her which slunk away when she went out into the world of people. Memories kept crowding her. Faces. That one face so like her own, that stared wildly out of a frame of murky water. Oh, *no! She* hadn't pushed her in! It was all Dan's doing. Dan ought to be the one who was haunted, wherever he was. In hell, perhaps.

Sometimes Dan would insist upon lying there on the floor in the dark beside her bed as he had been lying that night in the road when he was killed. There was blood on his head and it seemed to scream at her: "If you hadn't carried on the way you did Dan wouldn't have got so drunk and that accident wouldn't have happened." Myra always had to get up and turn on the light to make Dan go away.

Other times she thought she was fondling her own little boy in her arms. But he always woke up kicking and screaming for his daddy. Some times she was sure she was going mad. This Saturday evening was one of them.

When the last eater was filled, his scraps thrown away and his last dish washed and dried, Myra found herself seeking small chores to keep her from having to go out into the darkness to meet those terrible faces. But now the restaurant keeper was waiting to lock the kitchen. She had to put on her coat and leave. Yet she *would not* go to that room. The faces would be there.

The only face she thought she would have liked to see was that man who came and bamboozled her after Dan was killed. If it hadn't been for him she would still be on Easy Street enjoying Dan's money. If she could only find that man now she would scratch his eyes out. But what good would that do? She stepped down into a puddle and shivered as the cold muddy water seeped into her shoe.

Rain sought out the crevices in her clothing and worked its way through to her skin. In her weariness she was easily chilled. She tried to forget the rain. It was only water. Water couldn't hurt you. Water was good. There was plenty of water down by the bridge. Unconsciously her feet turned that way. Any way would do for her except the way to her room.

There were few people on the streets. Some distance ahead there was a bright neon sign: "JESUS SAVES." She read the words automatically. From long habit a sneer began to sweep them out of her mind. Then all at once she stopped and read them again. "JESUS SAVES." Did He? How could He?

She had reached the door of the little mission now and it was bright and warm in there. Just out of curiosity, to put off a little longer the time when she knew she would have to go back to her room, she pushed the door open and slipped into the back seat, half hidden behind a pile of extra chairs.

The room was well filled. Most of the audience were men, poor shipwrecked bums, some drunk, some asleep and giving a loud snore now and then. A few women were there. One was about her own age. The woman's face, in spite of deep marks of past sin, wore a bright look of peace. She smiled and handed Myra a hymnbook. They sang "The Old Rugged Cross." Myra hadn't heard that since she was a little girl. Then came a song that told about a "wonderful change wrought" in somebody's life "when Jesus came into his heart." Myra had a sudden wistful wonder whether such a change could ever come to her. Tears burned in her eyes but she blinked them back.

Then a man stood up on the platform and said, "Friends, we have a visitor here with us tonight, Roger Blackstone, a lawyer from Virginia. He has to hurry back so we are going to ask him to give us his testimony now. Roger, we're glad you stopped in."

The woman in the back seat clutched the chair ahead of her with both hands until the knuckles nearly burst the skin. Her eyes widened and she drew in her breath sharply. A tall lean young man, well dressed and poised in manner, smilingly stepped forward and spoke informally.

"I surely am glad to be able to say tonight that the Lord Jesus Christ is my Saviour. Maybe some of you men think that because I have on a whole suit of clothes I don't know what it is to go through hard times. But listen, fellows. When I was just a little kid I learned what it is to be without parents. My mother—

died,"—the woman in black gasped, clawed at her throat and slunk farther back behind the tower of chairs—"and my father was put in jail through no fault of his own. He is still there! It wasn't easy. But I want to tell you it's wonderful how the Lord planned for me and took care of me and saved me by His grace—because I was no angel, far from it!" Roger paused looking very serious. "And He has drawn me closer to Him through every trial I've had. He died for me and He means everything to me. I know He will save anybody who will do what I had to do, get down on my knees and admit that I was a sinner and needed Him for a Saviour. Boy! The peace that comes into your heart then is more than you can understand!" Roger gave a radiant smile. "I have to go now but I sure do hope somebody here gets to know Him tonight. Good-by, fellows!" He waved his hand to include them all and went out still smiling, as if he had not a care in the world.

Myra scarcely breathed while he spoke. Now she started to rise as if to follow him, then she sank back shaking with sobs and the tears streamed down her face. The woman who had handed her the book saw her distress and came and put her arm around her.

"Can I help you, dearie?" she said. "Do you know the Lord?"

Myra shook her head.

"Don't you want to, dearie?" she asked gently.

Myra lifted her poor twisting tormented face but she could not speak. She gave a pitiful nod.

"You come with me to the back room, dearie," said the kind-faced woman, and she led her away.

Two hours later, in speechless wonder, but with peace in her heart the woman who called herself Myra Foster walked quietly through the rain and the darkness to her room. She was not afraid of the faces any more. They were gone forever. Those people at the mission had explained that the blood of Jesus Christ had been shed for just such as she, and that God would never remind her of her sins through all eternity because of what Jesus Christ had done.

They had given her a little red book called "The Gospel of John" and, lest she lose the place, she still kept her finger on the verse that said, "He that believeth hath everlasting life and shall not come into condemnation." That was the weapon she intended to use against the faces if they dared to bother her again.

Tomorrow she would tell the restaurant manager that she was quitting and she would take the money she had scrimped to save and go to Virginia to see her son. Her son! He would tell her what to do to set things straight!

Sunday was another dreary day. A cold rain had started some time in the night and it drizzled at intervals all day.

Wynelle had hoped against hope that she would find a note under the screen showing that Roger was home. But there was none. She even put on her raincoat and galoshes and paddled outdoors and looked around on the ground for one lest the gusts of wind had blown it away. Disheartened, she went back into the house and sank down on the couch in the living room. It was very early in the morning, but she always hated to stay in bed when Mona was there, for she sprawled all over it; and especially when she had been out late at a dance the night before she was a most unpleasant bedfellow.

There were things that Wynelle knew she should do; a little mending for instance, for she was trying to keep her clothes going as long as possible so that she need spend no more of her small hoard. If she was to get only three dollars spending money a week it would be some time before she could afford anything new. But her heart was very heavy and the tears wanted to come again. She remembered last Sunday and what a happy time she had had. This was the day that Roger's father would be released. Had Roger forgotten? Or had he come home without getting in touch with her? She had the grace to feel ashamed of that last complaint. Why should she think he must let her know every time he stirred? She gave herself a shake and got up and went to the kitchen to get herself some breakfast. There was no use in fixing anything for the others. They would not be down for hours.

She had some thought of going to the little church where she had been last week with Roger, but even that did not stir her out of her discouragement. It was a long distance to walk and her foot would probably get to aching. She had strained it tramping so far yesterday. She ought not to afford a taxi, so there was no use attempting it.

She took her Bible after breakfast and tried not to shed tears as she thought longingly of the one who had given it to her. She could scarcely read the words for seeing his face between her and the page. She saw him laughing; she saw him grim and unsmiling as when he had looked at Richard that night when she fell and hurt her foot; she saw him as he had looked at her in the plane that first day when he told her to pray. At last, exasperated with herself, she closed the book and got up and put her clothes on. It was half past nine by that time, and she heard stealthy steps coming down the stairs. Thelma had heard her moving around.

Thelma in her childish cotton pajamas, with her owlish glasses off and her hair loose about her face was a much more attractive person than she usually was. Wynelle was surprised to see her.

"Are you going to church today?" Thelma asked abruptly. "I might as well go with you."

Wynelle had given up the idea altogether but now she thought perhaps she ought to try to go for the sake of this girl. She hesitated.

"I was afraid I couldn't walk that far," she confessed.

"There's a church two blocks from here," suggested Thelma as if she were recommending a grocery store and one was as good as another. "I've been a couple of times, years ago."

"Oh, is there?" responded Wynelle as brightly as she could. "Well, suppose we do, then."

Thelma nodded and, taking an apple, returned to her room to get ready.

Wynelle found herself not nearly so eager to go as she had been last Sunday, but she dutifully put on her navy suit and took her raincoat from the suitcase.

During the service she wondered whether there was something the matter with her. She simply could not get interested in what the minister was saying. His voice was merely a pleasant drone. She watched a fly walk up and down and across the back of a man's head in front of her, and her eyelids began to droop. She stole a look at Thelma who was sitting up stiffly without a sign of expression on her face. She wondered why the child had wanted to come. It was a relief when the meeting was over.

As they paddled drearily home in the driving rain, Thelma said in her usual sarcastic tone, "Well, that drip doesn't know what he's talking about, does he?"

Wynelle jerked wide awake.

"What do you mean?" she smiled amusedly.

"Why, giving out with all that rot about there being some good in everybody. That isn't what you told me. I've been watching you and comparing you to other people and I've decided that I'm going to believe what *you* say. I never saw anybody like you."

The speech was typical of Thelma, but its directness startled Wynelle. She gave a little embarrassed laugh.

"Why, I'm nothing at all," she cried. "I'm just as much a sinner inside as anybody else. I'm terribly ashamed of my thoughts sometimes."

"That may be," said Thelma, "but you don't swosh around in them like most people do. You have something most people don't have and I want it. If you aren't busy this afternoon I'd like you to take the Bible and teach me some more."

Wynelle gasped, amazed at the unspeakable joy that flooded her heart as she realized that this girl was really seeking the Lord as a result of her witness.

The day seemed to brighten perceptibly and Wynelle went about helping to get dinner, with a song in her heart and a prayer that she might not fail in the work she had been called upon to do that afternoon. She realized that it might mean eternal life or eternal death for the poor neglected child.

For two hours they pored over the Book together, following the notes that helped to explain what they read. Wynelle had a feeling that she learned more herself than Thelma did. It was not a wasted afternoon, at any rate.

At last Thelma drew a long deep sigh of relief.

"Well, I begin to see some things that I never understood," she said with a satisfaction in her tone that Wynelle had never heard there. "I'd like to do this again if you don't mind." She even had a meek and submissive note in her request that amazed Wynelle.

"I would too," she responded heartily. And as she went to her room to put away her Bible her eyes fell on the motto again. "Rejoice!" There was a way, then, to find joy in the midst of gloom.

She looked at the time. Five o'clock. Roger's father would be out by now. Had Roger come home in time to get him? Surely he would not have left his father to make his way home by himself! Why had he not got in touch with her? It did not seem like him. She felt as if she just must find out what was the matter. Tomorrow she would have to go back to that office that she hated, and work for the man whom she had learned to distrust completely. Perhaps she ought to quit right now and find a room just anywhere, and trust that she would get a job to pay her way before her last hundred dollars ran out. But suppose she didn't find a job? She couldn't do anything then but come trudging back to Snellers'. She couldn't write home for funds. She knew her mother had nothing, and her sister had none to spare, with the baby coming soon. The only other person she could appeal to was Roger and she could not bring herself to put any more burden on him with all his troubles. Anyway, he was a man and she was a girl and it just wouldn't be right to go to him for that kind of help. No, bad as things were it would be far worse to have to come

back to Snellers' and eat humble pie, and be given perhaps even less
than she had now. There was absolutely nothing for her to do
but go on as she was. But her prayers that night were desperate.

The next day she struggled half-heartedly through her work.
She had a feeling that every word she wrote might be incriminat-
ing in some way. The more so when she picked up the morning
paper and read that a probe of political activities was about to be
launched. Perhaps that man who was there Thursday would be
exposed, or even her cousin Dick! And then she might be called
upon to go to court and testify! Oh, what a mess everything was.
Why hadn't she stayed in Uniontown?

Perhaps if she went by bus she would still have enough money
to take her back. Maybe she ought to pack up and leave right
now. But the more she thought of doing that the more she realized
that her heart was here. She loved her little brown house, and
she loved—yes, she might as well admit it, she loved with all her
heart that young man who was living in it. She could not bear
to think of being thousands of miles away from him. She could
never forget that moment the Sunday before when he had looked
at her with his heart in his eyes. But if he cared why had he not
at least written her all these days? Well, there must be some good
reason. She would trust him. She had never found any reason not
to trust him.

The very realization, which she had never before faced, that she
loved Roger was enough to brighten the day for her in some
measure. There were still all sorts of questions hammering at her
mind, but she would wait, and somehow those questions would
be answered.

She forced herself to push on with her work, but she was fer-
vently thankful when the day at the office was over. Dick had
scarcely been civil. He was so irritable that she wondered sometimes whether he had discovered what she knew, but no, he
would have burst out at her in fury if he had. He was probably
just worried, as well he might be.

He went out early, as he did very often now, leaving Wynelle
to go home alone, which certainly was not displeasing to her. But
when she reached home and came to the dinner table she was
amazed at the change in him. He was in a very gay mood.

"Well," he announced beaming around on his family, "you are
eating dinner with the new Commonwealth Attorney. What do
you think of that?"

Alberta, who had evidently not been told the news, for Dick
always enjoyed having a large audience when he unveiled a surprise, dropped her knife and fork and stared at him. Wynelle
thought her cousin was about to cry for relief.

"Yes," he smiled blandly, "my election, they tell me, is certain."
Wynelle had the greatest difficulty in controlling her own expression lest the disgust she felt be apparent.

But the three older children were ecstatic, only Thelma retain-
ing her sardonic poise.

"Oh dad," cried Della, "can I have a convertible?"

Mona clasped her hands in a way she chose to use when she
wanted to register emotion, and exclaimed: "*Now* perhaps Emory
Ames will realize that this is a family worth marrying into."

And Richard said, "At last you will be able to give me a decent
job! I feel practically like a servant in that hotel. And now it's
going to be worse than ever. I go on night duty!" He groaned
under his burden.

Wynelle made an excuse to go into the kitchen to get the coffee.
She felt as if she could not stand facing them all one more minute.
She kept busy going back and forth the rest of the meal, waiting
on them. After dessert was finished Dick pushed back his chair
and said, "Don't worry if I'm late tonight, Alberta. They're having
a little get-together at the club for me." He turned from them
and straightened his tie in the mirror to hide a smile of self-
gratification.

A little later when he was about to leave the house, Wynelle,
doing the dishes in the kitchen, heard Alberta remind him to

take his raincoat, that the radio said a storm was due again.

She could hear him go to the closet and get it. He said, "Oh!" and then he came to the kitchen. Without apology he handed her a letter.

"This came for you last week," he said. "Alberta gave it to me to take to you at the office and I put it in the pocket of my raincoat and forgot it. Just came on it now."

He flung it down on the wet drainboard while Wynelle was drying her hands to take it, and went out.

Wynelle knew that handwriting and she opened the envelope eagerly. It was postmarked Chicago. She was glad that nobody was helping her with the dishes so that she had a few moments of privacy.

It was a note from Roger saying that he might not get home until nearly time to go for his father, and asking her if she would care to have him pick her up Sunday and take her out to the little brown house to prepare a nice homecoming dinner for his father.

"I know this is asking a lot, and you may not want to do it. If you don't I don't blame you. But you could probably think of ways to make it seem more like home than I could. If you want to do it call me at the house about one on Sunday and I'll come and get you. I doubt if I'll be home much before that.

"I'm enclosing a check in payment of my rent for last month and also for the coming month. We may find some other place for dad and me after that and you may be able to come in here with a friend yourself.

"I'll be counting on your prayers for dad. It won't be easy for him.

As ever your friend,
Roger."

Tears of disappointment were streaming down Wynelle's face by the time she finished that letter. It had been written on Wednesday of the week before. This was Monday night. What must he think of her? And how she would have *loved* to go over there

Sunday afternoon! That was something she could never regain. There would never be another homecoming like that. And to think that those two forlorn men had had to go home to an empty house on a dreary day to cook their own dinner. She felt as if she just couldn't stand it that Roger had wanted her and she had not come. It was a temptation actually to hate the man who had been the cause of it.

Then all at once she remembered the talk she had had with Thelma. Could it be that it was not her cousin's fault but that the Lord had arranged the day for her? An unexpected gladness stole into her heart at the thought. Nevertheless, her impulse was to phone Roger immediately and explain to him. How disappointed he must have been when she did not call! She glanced at the clock. In a few minutes most of the family would be gone. There would not be so many inquisitive ears to pry into her telephone conversation.

She hurried through the rest of the kitchen work, which the others were finding more and more excuses to leave to her.

As she dried the last of the dishes she planned what she would say, and her heart was pounding with eagerness to hear Roger's voice again.

She waited until they had all gone out except the two younger girls and their mother. They were upstairs and wouldn't hear. She felt as if she simply could not wait any longer.

But she dialed and dialed and there was no answer.

Then the doorbell rang and she went to the door. Two big policemen walked in and looked sternly at her.

CHAPTER 21

SUNDAY AFTERNOON WAS a dark time for Roger Blackstone. He reached home about noon and busied himself preparing something for dinner in anticipation of his father's homecoming. His nerves were on edge for the telephone. Every minute he expected it would ring, and he would hear Wynelle's voice. His heart turned over with eagerness each time he thought of it.

But the call did not come. He put off as long as possible the setting of the table, hoping that at least she would come in time to perform that little service, for he was aware that his own efforts at homemaking did not measure up to the standards of Gram Williams. Wynelle would probably have thought of little things to do. She'd put flowers somewhere, and maybe bake muffins or something, instead of using the plain cold loaf of bread. He had spread a clean cloth on the little dinette table, which he usually left bare when he was alone, and he had laid out Gram Williams' best china and silver. But still there was a barrenness about the arrangements that left him disconsolate. Why didn't Wynelle call?

At last he had to take his car and go off alone to the prison. It was hard to believe that this would be his last trip.

"Wish I had a dollar for every time I've been through those ugly doors!" he muttered to himself as he drew up and parked. Then he felt the despair of the place drench him as it always did when he entered. He was getting his father out of there today, but what about the other poor souls who weren't going to get out? And how was his father much better off if his body was free but his soul was not? He flung yet another prayer heavenward that his father might be saved.

Their conversation on the way home was sparse. Mr. Blackstone glanced about him at the landscape, familiar fifteen years ago, and now so changed.

"Does it look good to you, dad?" Roger questioned hopefully.

Morton grunted and shrugged. "Yes and no," he replied noncommittally. Roger sighed. There was a sort of anticlimax about this moment for which they both had waited so long. It was flavorless and dull.

As they drew near the little brown house Roger wondered whether Wynelle would be there to surprise him. But he opened the door and the same old unpeopled silence greeted him. His heart sank. He had not realized how very much he had hoped she would be there.

The rain began to beat again outside. The skies were very dark. Something had gone wrong with the kitchen light and he had to bring in the little table lamp from the living room. It cast strange shadows and the place did not seem like home. He gave a stir to the stew he had put on before he left. He wanted to phone Wynelle but he wouldn't. He had left her free to come or stay and she had stayed. He would have to let it go at that.

His father showed no eagerness about anything. He sat down in a chair before the fireplace and picked up a newspaper. He kept glancing about nervously, but that was all the sign he gave that he had not been in this house waiting for dinner every Sunday for the past fifteen years. To Roger it seemed a strange reaction.

At dinner his father was in his usual bitter mood, not at all elated by his freedom. Roger tried his best to cheer him, but as a matter of fact his own thoughts were busy struggling to reconcile himself to the thought that Wynelle was out of his life permanently. It did not seem reasonable that anything would have kept her from calling him unless she was done with him. He had dreamed that some day they might live together in the little brown house that they both loved so much. He shut his lips firmly and swallowed hard. His disappointment was keen.

He watched the rain spatter down beyond the bright yellow curtains, and bravely made another attempt to start a conversation.

"It's good to have you back, dad." He tried to sound spontaneous. His father only grunted assent.

"Lucky we could rent this little house for a while." He had already explained the arrangements to his father.

"Yes," agreed Morton and went on eating.

Roger started to say that he was glad the old house had been torn down. Then he decided not to mention it. He thought of telling about Della's accident. But that would bring up the Sneller family, and that wouldn't be good. There was some prohibition on every subject, it seemed. This was deadly! A whole afternoon of it was not pleasant to look forward to.

Sometimes he caught a wild look of frenzy in his father's face but it would soon fade into his usual dejection. Just once he looked up and found his father's eyes upon him compassionately, almost lovingly. That one glance gave him a ray of hope.

They cleared away the dishes and sat down to read. The whole afternoon was gloomy.

Roger tried talking about the work at the hotel which his father was to start the next day. Mr. Blackstone only looked at him coldly and then looked away.

Roger finally suggested that they go to the evening church service. His father did not refuse so they went, but Roger was fairly desperate. He wondered whether his father's mind was already so far gone that he would not be able to do the work at the hotel.

People stared curiously at the tall young man with the uncompromising jaw and the dejected bitter-looking man who was with him. Most of them knew Roger. Some knew his father. One or

two elderly ladies came over to speak and smiled at Mr. Blackstone. One said with probably good intention that she "hoped
he was going to do better now." Roger writhed at that, but his
father only looked dully resentful and did not answer.

The old crippled minister was most cordial, however, and did
much to ease the tension in Roger's soul. He took Mr. Blackstone
by the hand as if he were a dear old friend and welcomed him
among them.

"I hope we shall see a lot of you," he said genially. "We think
a great deal of your fine boy, and I've been looking forward to
getting really well acquainted with his father. I would like to
have been over to see you oftener," he added, as if Mr. Blackstone
had been spending his vacation in a neighboring inn, "but this
business of not being able to make my own way about is a great
hindrance!" He laughed light-heartedly, pointing to his useless
limb.

Roger let his gratitude to the old man shine in his face. His
father looked up in surprise and a glimmer of interest appeared in
his dull eyes, but then he looked away again as if what he had
heard could not be true.

"Bring your father to see me, Roger," said the minister with
warmth. "Often!" he added with a look that showed his sincerity.

With that small balm Roger took his father back to the little
brown house and they went to bed. But Roger lay awake a long
time going over all the problems that seemed to present themselves to him in a continual procession. He faced the probability
of having to move out of this dear place that had been home to
him almost ever since he could remember. It was not that he
cared so much about leaving it, but the thought that it belonged
to Wynelle and she had not cared to call him, was like a con-
tinuous painful weight on his mind. He tried to shake it off but
he could not. He knew that the girl who had walked so trustfully
into his arms that day on the plane had become the dearest thing

in life to him. If she did not care for him, that could not be helped. In fact, he didn't see why she would. But he knew that he would never change, that there would never be another girl for him.

He forced his mind back to the problem of the woman in Chicago. It was important, now that he had most of the rest of his facts in line, that he did not lose sight of her. She must be available to him at any moment. He wondered for the hundredth time what effect it would have upon his father when the fact of his innocence was made public. He did not dare to bring it up until the right psychological moment.

Toward morning he fell asleep but when it was time to get up he was not rested. He took his father to his work at the Maple Grove Inn and left him but not without many a qualm. He promised to come back that evening and pick him up.

It was a temptation all day long to call Wynelle at Dick's office. But he not only disliked having to talk to her there where every word might be censored, but he had persuaded himself that she didn't care to go on with him. He argued the matter back and forth with himself but he did not call.

He worked late at his office. Just before he went out to his solitary dinner in Middle City the telephone rang. It was his detective friend in Chicago to say that "Myra Foster" had taken a train for Washington Sunday night.

Roger frowned as he hung up. Now what did that mean? He put a Washington detective on the case and went out to dinner, after which he drove slowly back to Maple Grove.

The air was heavy and humid, breathing that sense of impending disaster that often seems to hang in the atmosphere before a storm. He could scarcely suppress a groan of discouragement as he rode along. Then all at once from somewhere in his mind came the thought of that motto he had made with such care for Wynelle. He had insisted to her that there was joy to be found in even the fiercest of trials. Where was his joy now? He drew up at the side of the road and put his head across his arms on the wheel.

"Oh God," he cried aloud, "forgive me for feeling sorry for myself when You have done so much for me! Show me how to glorify You in the fire. And work out all these things the way You want them, not my way. Do it for the sake of Your Son, because He died for me."

Several minutes he paused there alone in the darkness. Then with his heart considerably lighter he drove on to the hotel to pick up his father. But he had not yet reached the building when he saw his father come staggering down the street.

The hotel lobby was quiet. No guests were on hand to notice the gray-haired middle-aged man with the odd-looking haircut come stumbling in haste down the carpeted stairs.

Richard Sneller was leaning sentimentally over the shoulder of the pretty telephone operator as if trying to read something printed on a card she held. In reality he was telling her what lovely hair she had and she blushed and giggled. They were much absorbed in one another. Richard turned but he gave only half his attention to the man who stopped at the desk and tremblingly stammered in a hollow voice:

"Two eighteen! Two eighteen! Get up there quick!" and then almost ran out of the hotel.

Richard finished what he had been saying to the girl before the words sank into his consciousness. Gradually the silly look faded from his face. Who was that man? He reminded him of someone. He acted daffy. But just in case he wasn't it would be well to check on two eighteen.

"Sam!" he called under his breath to the gangling-legged black boy who lounged on the bell boys' bench. Sam's eyes rolled around in his head like marbles.

"Yas suh?"

"Get up to two eighteen and see what gives!"

"Yas suh!" Sam lurched off.

In half his usual errand time he was back panting, his eyeballs rolling white. In a sepulchral whisper he said to Richard:

"Dat two eighteen she need a doctor quick. Or a nambulance, maybe."

Richard, frightened at last, gave instructions to the pretty operator. The doctor from five one four was called. After a few moments an ambulance clanged at the hotel's back door. Then all was quiet as usual in the lobby.

Roger stopped the car and opened the door.

"Get in, dad," he called.

His father gazed wildly up at him. He tried to say something but his jaw only quivered and the words would not come.

"Get in, dad," commanded Roger gently again.

But his father stood there and shook his head as if he hadn't heard him.

Roger got out and took him by the arm to put him into the car.

"Come on, dad, it's time to go home," urged Roger patiently as if he were dealing with a little child.

"No!" answered his father hoarsely. "No! I can't! I've got to go back!"

"Back where, dad?"

"Back to the prison."

Roger's heart sank.

"No, dad. You're done with that now. You are to come home with me." He started to pull him gently toward the car.

"No, you don't understand!" spoke his father in a hollow tone. "I've *done* it! I didn't do it before. But I've done it now."

"Come, dad," persisted Roger, wondering whether he ought to take his father to a doctor right away.

But his father looked him straight in the eye under the street light and said:

"Roger boy—" He choked. "Son, I've—I've *killed* your mother."

"*Dad!*" Roger swayed as if he had been struck. "Oh *dad!*" he moaned.

"I—I didn't *mean* to kill. I don't know what possessed me. I hope they kill *me,* son," his father said hoarsely. "I deserve it! Take me back, son!"

"Oh—*God!*" cried Roger under his breath. His mouth was dry. He was shaking all over. "Get in, dad," he commanded.

"I've got to go back, son. Will you take me back?" his father begged tremblingly.

"Yes, yes, dad, but tell me about it first."

His father climbed into the car and slumped down, his head in his hands. He gripped his hair in both hands as if he would pull it out.

"Tell me! Quick!" insisted Roger as he started the car.

His father looked up at him, his face ghastly in the pale light. "She was there, in the hotel!"

"Yes, I know, dad."

"You *know?*"

"Well, I knew she was in Washington. I can understand that she might have come here. I was going to tell you she was alive as soon as I could get the case reopened. You would have been *cleared,* dad! Oh, why didn't I tell you before!" The remorse in Roger's tone was heartrending.

But his father did not seem to take in what Roger said.

"She walked through the lobby," he continued in a dazed way, "and I knew her right away. She looked old but I knew her. I followed her upstairs to her room. I—I think I must have been crazy! I slid in the door after her and faced her. She was frightened and started to scream. Before I knew it I struck her and the next thing I knew she went limp and fell on the floor! Oh God! What possessed me? Every step I followed her I kept thinking of all those years, the hell she put us through, you and me! Something came into my hands. I don't know what it was. Hate, perhaps. Son, I'm a—a murderer! Oh *God!* All these years I've been so sure I would never do such a thing! Take me back, son, and turn me in! I'm not fit to live any more!"

Wrenched with horror, Roger tried to think what to do. He knew that the penitentiary was not the place to go.

"We'll have to report it first, dad," he said huskily. It was hard to control the trembling of his voice.

"Yes," agreed Morton, "I don't want to run away, son."

Roger thought he never had loved his father as he did now, in spite of the horror that clawed at his heart. All of a sudden he found a fierce pleasure in being able to stand by him, a pleasure he never had felt all those years when his father was innocent. He couldn't understand it. As long as his father had tried to justify himself he had helped him from a sense of duty. Now that he was laid low nothing could have induced Roger to desert him.

Desperately he tried to decide what to do. "We'll go to the police court," he said finally. "There is a big crime probe on and the Commonwealth Attorney may be there tonight."

CHAPTER 22

WYNELLE'S EYES GREW wide with consternation when she realized that the policemen were looking at her so accusingly. Could it be that they had found out about what Cousin Dick had done and she was going to be held, too, because she had not immediately reported what was on that record? Her hand went up to her throat in a little frightened gesture and instantly the look on the two officers' faces became even more stern.

"Are you Della Sneller?" asked one of them, looking at a paper he held in his hand.

"No," replied Wynelle wonderingly.

"You're *not?*" insisted the officer severely.

Wynelle wanted to giggle in her nervousness.

"No, of course not," she answered again.

"Do you know Della Sneller? Is she here?"

"Yes, I think she is. I'll call her," said Wynelle, going to the foot of the stairs. She started up but Della had heard the bell and, thinking it to be her escort of the evening, she was already on her way down, looking very plump and gay in a bright red evening dress and little gold slippers.

When her eyes fell on the two burly men awaiting her she gave a startled scream and turned back.

But one of the men took a step after her.

"Here, miss!" he commanded. "Come back here. Are you Della Sneller?"

Della dissolved in loud sobs and the officer had to appeal to Wynelle for confirmation. She nodded, half reluctantly. She had a

217

feeling that she was being put in the position of informing on her relatives.

One of the officers had Della by the arm now and was starting the rest of the way down the stairs with her. Her scream had brought her mother to the scene, but Alberta was not much of a power without her husband to back her up. She remonstrated tearfully and then she too began to wring her hands and cry.

"I'm sure there's some mistake, officer,." she insisted. "I wish you would wait until I can call my husband. He is a lawyer, you know, and he would know what to do. In fact," she added, drawing herself up proudly, "he is to be elected the new Commonwealth Attorney." She took on an indignant tone full of rebuke, at which the two policemen exchanged a significant look. "I'm afraid that you will find yourselves in a very unpleasant position if you take my daughter away like this."

"Lady," replied the officer unfeelingly, "I have a warrant here to bring your daughter for questioning. The Gilkie girl died tonight and that's the usual procedure." Della gave another terrified scream, but he went relentlessly on. "I've got nothin' to do with it. It's my orders. Sorry, lady. Come miss, you better go quietly."

Della choked down her sobs and put her hands out to Wynelle.

"Can't you go wi-ii-ith me?" Della wailed. "Don't leave me to go off to that terrible place all a-lo-o-one!"

The officers looked at one another and the taller one nodded. "I s'pose she can go if you want 'er. May be a long time, though." But Alberta put in again, fearfully.

"Officers, I insist that you let me call my husband before you take that child away from me."

Exasperated, they agreed.

"Okay, lady, call 'im. But get a hustle on."

Alberta went to the phone. She was so distraught, however, that she could not think how to look up the number of Dick's club.

Wynelle found it for her, but when a man answered he said that Dick was not there.

"Why," insisted Alberta, "I understood that he was to have a little party there tonight!"

"Oh?" answered the man. "Oh! Why, yes! He's having a little party all right." He gave an ugly laugh. "But it's not here. You better call the police court. Everybody's over there tonight."

She called the police court and demanded to talk to her husband. There seemed to be quite a discussion over whether he could come to the phone or not but at last with great relief she heard his voice.

"Well?" he said uncivilly.

"Oh Dick!" she cried breaking down again, "there are two policemen here who are trying to take Della with them. They say Nancy Gilkie died. Dick, can't you come and tell them not to?"

For answer Dick swore roundly, then he fairly roared:

"No! I can't! I'm in a hell of a mess myself. Della got herself into that jam by disobeying me and she can get herself out of it." And he slammed the receiver down.

Alberta collapsed in sobs, crying, "Oh, my child, my darling child!" as the policemen stalked out of the house with Della between them. "Oh, you go with her, won't you?" she appealed to Wynelle. "I declare, I don't know what we're coming to!"

Wynelle, hardly knowing what she should do, or how she could help, went out after them. But just as she closed the door she heard Thelma say to her mother, "Well, *I* know what we're coming to. The Bible tells it very plainly. Get up, mother, and let's get your psychons straightened out."

Wynelle could not repress a little chuckle all to herself. Thelma was "different," to say the least, but she might amount to something some time.

Wynelle put her arm about the weeping Della in the police car and wondered at herself. Here she was two thousand miles from what was supposed to be her home, walking straight into the meshes of a case of manslaughter. What good could she possibly do? All she would accomplish, likely, would be to get herself into some very unsavory limelight. Still she felt sorry for Della. She realized more than ever tonight how very little the child had ever had of a stable moral background. She had certainly made a tangle of her short life. And as far as Wynelle could see, she was about as defenseless as an oyster without its shell, especially if her father didn't help her.

They drove quickly through the wet streets and fresh sobs came from Della as they drew up in front of a brightly lighted building that seemed to be quite a rendezvous this evening, judging by the number of cars parked in front.

As they got out and went into the building Wynelle thought she caught a glimpse of a coupe that looked like Roger's. But of course there must be more than one little car like his in the town.

She followed the policemen and Della into the big square room on the right and there he was!

Her heart gave a great leap of joy and then seemed to stop still for an instant. She had never seen Roger look as he did now. His face was pale as chalk, and his eyes were small points of burning fire. But they were steady and his chin was up. His back was straight as an arrow, as if he were going into battle. His father stood close behind him trying to master his shaking limbs.

Roger was speaking to one of the officers near the door as if he had just come in and was telling his errand. He did not see Wynelle. The room was thick with smoke.

There was an altercation going on at the far side of the room. Loud voices, angry cursing, even a fist raised. Wynelle caught sight of the politician who had been in Dick's office on Thursday, and then she saw Dick himself, red with mortification and glowering in rage. There were several other men there whom she did not know.

Apparently the graft probe storm had broken, but why was Roger mixed up in it all? He had evidently made the officer to whom he had been speaking understand that his errand was urgent, for he was led straight up to the Chief's desk. The officer broke through the angry, gesticulating crowd and said a few words to the man seated behind the desk who rapped for order and gave commands to the police sergeant. The combatants seemed loath to quiet down but in a few moments they were drawn off to one side and hushed. Roger and his father, oblivious of the crowd or of personalities, took their stand before the Chief, an elderly man named Johnson.

Della was casting frightened glances about the room between her sobs. A policeman told her to "Sit here, miss!" and planted both her and Wynelle in chairs against the wall near the desk.

Wynelle could have reached out and touched Roger, she was so close to him. She could see his fist clenched till it was white at the knuckles. He was trying to control his breathing, groping for words to begin his story.

The Chief looked up at Roger with respect. He seemed to be acquainted with him.

Wynelle had a sudden recollection of the moment when Roger had jumped with her from the plane. How safely he had held her then. She wished that she could impart to him the same sense of comfort and comradeship now, for he was obviously in distress.

Roger hesitated only a moment. Then in a low tone he stated his father's case briefly. There was electric silence in the room as he finished.

Mr. Johnson studied the trembling old man. Although Morton Blackstone was only fifty-odd he looked twenty years more than that now.

"But Blackstone," the puzzled Chief demurred, addressing Roger, "there must be some mistake!"

"Yes sir," returned Roger. "There *was,* a great mistake. But it was made fifteen years ago. I have always known that my father was innocent of the crime, and I had only this week uncovered full proof to that effect. I was planning to appeal for the case to be reopened."

The Chief frowned in perplexity. Then with an astonishing lack of severity he indicated that Roger and his father should be seated pending an investigation, and he gave orders that a checkup be made immediately.

Morton slumped down with his face in his hands. Roger took a seat beside him, looking straight ahead and seeing nothing. Dick had paused in his loud justification of his own evildoing long enough to listen to the strange story with a sneer of contempt on his florid face. Della had been too busy to notice, for she was trying to attract the attention of Ted who had just been brought in and was lolling in his chair attempting to appear unconcerned. Many of the other spectators had already begun to buzz with gossip, especially the older ones who recalled the trial of Morton Blackstone fifteen years ago.

A reporter saw his chance and approached Roger to question him.

Wynelle sat white and tense, her icy hands clenched together, her heart torn with anguish for the man she loved. She saw Roger, after three attempts, succeed in waving away the reporter, who immediately took off for the oldest man in the room to get the story from him.

The politicians began their controversy again. Della still waited. Her father paid no attention to her. Perhaps he did not even know that she was in the room.

Wynelle could not keep her eyes from Roger. His face stood out in contrast to the other men in the room. She exulted in his clean-cut look, the strength of purpose in the lines about his mouth, the straight-forwardness of his bearing. But the suffering in his face cut her to the heart. He was sitting on the opposite side of the room with his head leaning wearily back against the wall. His eyes were closed. Now and then his lips seemed to move. Wynelle guessed that he was praying.

Finally she could restrain herself no longer. Crowd or no crowd she got up and walked across to him, taking the vacant seat beside him. She laid her hand gently on his arm.

He opened his eyes and looked at her in amazement. He did not smile, his anguish was too deep for that. But his tortured eyes thanked her for coming.

"How did you know?" he asked in a low agonized tone.

"I didn't," she said. "I came with Della." She pointed over to where the girl waited disconsolately, mopping her bloated face occasionally. "The girl who was hurt died tonight and they brought Della here for questioning."

Roger shook his head commiseratingly. "Della too? It's strange, isn't it!"

"No. 'Beloved, think it not strange,'" she quoted softly. All at once a slow smile like the lighting of a lamp transformed Roger's face. He seized her hand and gave it a quick squeeze.

"Thanks, for reminding me. I should be ashamed of myself."

Wynelle gave him a comradely grin. "I admit it does seem strange that Della and her father should land here both at once, though, doesn't it?" she said. "I guess he is in real financial trouble, too. But that's nothing compared to your trouble. Please don't hesitate to call on me if there's anything I can do. I want you to know that I didn't get your letter about Sunday until this evening. I was heartbroken. I would have loved to do that! I tried to call you tonight."

"Oh, that!" he smiled sadly. "Well, it was all right. I missed you, though. But it's great having you turn up just now. Thanks a million. It isn't everybody who would be willing to come and sit down here with us, you know."

"Why what do you mean?" cried Wynelle.

"It was bad enough before. It will be worse now."

Wynelle shook her head. "I don't see why. I think it's easy to see why your father would feel frantic with hate. A woman who let you both go through all that—" She spoke heatedly but suddenly she broke off, mortified to realize that she was speaking about Roger's mother.

"It's okay," he assured her, sadly. "And there's no excuse for what dad did."

"But I can understand it," Wynelle said earnestly.

Roger looked at her in wonder.

"You always understand, don't you?" he said gratefully.

Just then the officers returned who had been sent out to the Inn. Roger's name was called. Wynelle returned to Della's side. The same hush settled down on the room.

Mr. Johnson asked a few more questions of Roger's father whose answers could scarcely be heard.

Then the Chief spoke with finality.

"We have checked your story, Mr. Blackstone." He paused. Everyone seemed to hold his breath. Then Mr. Johnson went on in stern, measured tones. "Your wife is in the hospital, very ill, but she will live. You may go!"

Everybody gasped in astonishment. The talk buzzed. Some cheered. Some ranted. Some gossiped.

Tears rained down Wynelle's cheeks. She saw the puzzled relief on Roger's face. Suddenly he turned to her and gave his wonderful smile, with a grateful glance upward. Then he put his arm around his father to lead him out.

But before they reached the door Mr. Johnson's tired voice could be heard setting the bail for Della at one thousand dollars.

Roger stopped and came back. He walked straight up to Dick Sneller who glared at him hatefully.

Everyone quieted again to listen.

"I would like to put up the bond for your daughter, sir," said Roger. He stooped to the desk and wrote a check while Dick, overcome with astonishment, stared at him.

But when Roger handed him the check his face turned purple.

He tore the check across and threw the pieces on the floor at Roger's feet.

"My daughter will go to jail before I'll take such help!" he roared. He was about to strike Roger but two officers seized his wrists.

Roger looked him steadily in the eye a moment, then picked up the two halves of his check, stuffed them in his pocket and went out amid a storm of boos aimed at Dick.

Outside, the father and son stood facing each other a moment before they got into the car.

Roger stood tall and straight but his father still looked shrunken.

"It will always be like that!" groaned Morton.

"What if it is?" answered Roger calmly. "That can't hurt us. God has been good to us, dad."

"God?" muttered the older man. "God? How could He ever have anything to do with me? I committed a murder in my heart."

"Yes, dad, I know that," replied Roger soberly. "But there is a point of law called double jeopardy, which means that a person can't be punished twice for the same crime. Even if she hadn't lived it's possible they couldn't have held you."

His father shook his head. "It doesn't sound right, son," he insisted.

"Well, come with me, dad. We'll talk to Dr. Anderson." Roger put him into the car and they drove to old Dr. Anderson's house.

CHAPTER 23

AT MIDNIGHT ROGER and his father were still seated around the fire in the home of the old crippled minister. Dr. Anderson had listened to the whole story, watching their faces compassionately. There was a long silence after they had finished. Dr. Anderson sat with his head bowed, his thin wrinkled hand across his brow as if he were suffering with them. At last he looked up, straight at Morton.

"'There is therefore now *no* condemnation to them that are in Christ Jesus,'" he quoted softly.

Morton looked puzzled.

"Oh, but that's just it, Doctor," he said. "I feel terribly condemned. I never did before because I was innocent. Now," he groaned wretchedly, "I'm not!"

Dr. Anderson shook his head. "You weren't innocent before either," he said. The words were cruelly startling. "My friend," reasoned the old man gently, "is the desire to murder the only one of the ten commandments that you ever broke?"

"Why no, I don't suppose it is," answered Morton. "But it's the worst."

"Possibly. But did you ever realize that God has said that if you break one you are guilty of all?"

"No, I never did."

The minister reached for his worn Bible on a little table beside him. "God knows our stubborn old hearts," he said, "and He knows that sometimes we won't admit that we need to be saved until we go the limit in sin. He allows us to be tested at the very

226

point at which we think we are strongest. Then we fall and we cry out to Him as He wants us to do. Isn't that so?"

"I guess it is," confessed the poor man shamefacedly.

"You'd like a clear conscience again, wouldn't you?"

"*Would* I!" cried Morton in desperation. "But that will never be."

"It will if you take God's Son as your Saviour. That's the only way any of us ever got rid of the burden of sin."

"You mean that this feeling of being a criminal would be gone?" queried Morton. He was pitifully in earnest.

"That's just what I mean. He will forgive and forget. Listen." The old minister turned the leaves of his Book. " 'Your sins . . . will I remember no more.' That's because His Son took the guilt of them. The penalty *has already been paid!*"

For the first time a glimmer of hope dawned in Morton's eyes. Several minutes he sat in deep thought. Then like a child he went down on his knees and a sob broke from him that came from the depths of his heart.

"Oh Lord!" he said brokenly, "I'm an awful sinner. I guess You have always known it, but I was too blind to see it. Forgive me and save me."

A light of glory shone through the tears in Dr. Anderson's eyes as he said, " 'Whosoever shall call upon the name of the Lord shall be saved.' Get up, Morton, 'There is . . . *no* condemnation.' "

Peace settled upon Morton's tired features as he arose from his knees.

"I see it now!" he exclaimed. "And the burden *is* gone! Thank the Lord! Now I'd like to go back and tell some of those other fellows in the pen."

Roger was radiant as he watched his father's transformation.

Mrs. Anderson came smiling in just then with a tray.

"Come here, mother," called her husband, "and meet a new member of the Family, 'a child of God by faith in Christ Jesus!' "

She set down the tray and folded Morton's big calloused hand in her soft ones.

"The Lord bless you," she said softly with love in her eyes.

Morton had to wipe glad tears away. "I didn't know it could ever be like this again!" he said. "Why, I really have peace in my heart! I can't understand it. And you act as if you—*loved* me!"

"Morton," smiled the old minister, "you'll find more love among the children of God than you ever knew existed in this world. Not all of them will show it of course, for many are just babes and don't know yet how to love, but the ones who walk close to Him will love you. They will be glad to wipe out the past. Now let's thank Him."

He bowed his head and talked very simply to the Heavenly Father, commending the newborn babe to His care.

But Morton could scarcely taste his tea and cookies. He sat and stared around at the Andersons. Finally he said, "If anybody had told me two hours ago that I would ever be this happy again I would have said they were crazy! I can't take it in!"

"'The peace that passeth understanding!'" murmured Mrs. Anderson lovingly.

Dr. Anderson gave them a smile like a blessing when they said good night. "The Lord bless you both," he called after them.

When they reached home the telephone was ringing wildly. Roger's thoughts immediately rushed to Wynelle. Perhaps there was more trouble at the Snellers'. He was so elated over what had just happened to his father that he felt as if he wanted to help the whole world, even the Snellers.

He took off the receiver.

"Mr. Blackstone?" a woman's relieved voice called. "This is the Maple Grove Hospital. A patient named Myra Foster is calling for you. She has been conscious for two hours and we have been trying to locate you."

Roger caught his breath. "I'll be right down," he gasped.

Whirling to his father he seized him by the arms. "Dad!" He almost wept. "Come on!"

They rushed out to the car.

"Oh, but God is good to us!" exclaimed Roger breathlessly as they tore through the quiet streets.

Morton hesitated.

"Yes, son, He is. I don't deserve it. But even though He has kept her alive, that doesn't make it any better, what I did!" There was immeasurable sadness in his tone. Roger could have wept for him.

"I know, dad," he agreed huskily. "But you've got to remember that God has wiped out all that. In His sight you're just as if you'd never done it."

"That's hard to realize. I believe it, but I've asked Him never to let me forget that I'm capable of it, or of any sin in the list. I never knew that was true but it is."

"We all are, dad," said Roger soberly. "It's only His grace that keeps us from the gutter! Lots of people won't agree to that but it's so. The Book says it. And I guess you and I *know* it now."

They drew up at the hospital, suddenly aware of a great reluctance to go in.

"I—I'm going to ask her to forgive me," said Morton. "I'm not going to think any more of all she did to us. That's past. It's strange, but all the bitterness I felt toward her is gone. If God can forgive me, I guess I can forgive her."

"Okay, dad," said Roger, and again that rush of love swept over him. It was going to be great to have a real father again, one he could respect.

But as for himself, it was one of the hardest things he had ever had to do, to approach that bed where his mother lay with white face and closed eyes. For many years he had counted her out of his thoughts. It was difficult to realize that he was going to have to reckon on her again. He had no sweet and precious memories of her. What would she be like now? This reunion might not be easy to take in stride.

Morton's heart was wrung. He found himself comparing this worn gray-haired woman with the wife he had known. He studied her face. She was pitifully thin and sad. All the flippancy was gone. She reminded him more of the young girl he had loved than of the hard-hearted woman who had run off and left him to suffer. Now it seemed as if all he could think of was the time he had first taken her in his arms.

All at once she opened her eyes and saw him. Relief and remorse flooded her face.

"Morton!" She lifted a weak hand. "Can you forgive me?"

In an instant he was on his knees beside her. "Yes, oh yes!" he cried softly. "And you?"

"I didn't blame you, Morton. I've been *awful!* A terrible sinner. But Morton, God has forgiven me! Roger!" She motioned for him to come near. "Oh, my boy!" The tears drenched her face. "It was you who showed me the way back. It's all different now. I'm glad God let me live to tell you this."

Wonderingly Roger came to the edge of the bed.

"I was there last Saturday night," she went on. "At the mission. I was afraid you would see me. I was almost ready to take my life. And then you spoke about Jesus and He seemed to be right there. He put out His arms and said He'd forgive me and I could start again. Oh, I've sinned, I've sinned! But He has washed it all away. Can you both forgive me?"

It seemed to Roger as if songs were filling the air. The very room was bright. His throat felt tight but it was joy that choked him.

"Oh, mother!" he cried brokenly. "I didn't know you were there!" It seemed a stupid thing to say when there was so much to be said, but his mother understood. A smile of peace was on her face.

"Myrtle," said Morton still holding her hand tenderly, "God

has saved me, too. He is a *wonderful* Saviour. We don't deserve any of this. I never knew what He could do. Everything's so different."

"Yes," agreed his wife. "So different. So wonderful. Oh, it's been—hell! I wanted to come back years ago but my awful pride wouldn't let me. Morton, do you know what I did?"

"Never mind, Myrtle," he soothed. "Don't try to talk now."

"Yes, I want to tell you both. I want to have it all out and be done with it forever. Then we can start fresh. It was Dan Winters, you know." She spoke with great effort as if the very memories were burning wounds. "He kept coming. He would buy me things. I knew he was married, to my twin sister. You never knew I had a sister, did you, Morton? They lived in Seattle. We were identical, except that Myra was quiet. Dan said he liked lively girls and he wanted me. He had money and I wanted money. I was crazy and foolish. I know that now. He came that time you were away so long and insisted that I go off with him. Myra had guessed that there was a woman and she followed him. We had an awful quarrel, all of us. Finally we sort of patched it up, and Dan suggested that we go out in the boat. I knew what he had in mind, for he had told me. I shouldn't have given in. I don't know what possessed me! But I did. I loaned Myra my clothes to go out in the boat. That was part of the plan. We got out to the middle of the lake and—and Dan—oh! I've never forgotten it. It was terrible!"

Morton held her hand gripped tightly in his. There was no bitterness any more in his heart, only a great relief that the truth was coming out at last and in such a way.

"We went off together that night. It was easy to be Myra. Too easy! No one saw us. You weren't expected back till the next day. I wish you had come, only I don't suppose that would have made any difference, the way I was then. I was bent on having all the money I wanted. Dan had made it in oil. He bought me everything. We traveled. For a while I thought I was happy.

But I never could forget. Dan and I quarreled a lot. One night we quarreled in the car. He was pretty drunk. We smashed up and he was killed. I had all his money then and I went to town with it! But I still wasn't happy. Another man came along after that and I thought I loved him. He got all the money from me and left. I've been almost penniless now for three years. It's good I was, or I never would have gone into the mission that night. Thank God I was at the end of my rope!"

Roger had not taken his eyes off his mother while she talked. He felt weak all over with relief. Everything she said proved what he had already discovered. But how marvelously God had taken the whole case right out of his hands! There would be no need now to reopen it.

The nurse came in finally and sent them home.

Morton patted his wife's hand. "We'll be in again," he promised. "And you are not to worry. Everything is going to work out all right. Good night." He bent and kissed her forehead.

The little brown house was dark when they reached home. Roger switched on the light and all the dear familiar objects seemed to greet him.

As simply as children father and son knelt down in the kitchen by the bright little dinette table and gave thanks for the victories wrought that day.

CHAPTER 24

THE SNELLER HOUSEHOLD was in a turmoil. It was late when Wynelle and Della got home. Dick had had difficulty arranging for bail. Mrs. Sneller was frantic. Thelma seemed to be at her wits' end.

Wynelle noticed the change in Thelma immediately. She seemed to have grown up in the few hours since they had left with the police. She waited on them all, getting them something hot to drink, turning down their beds, trying to comfort her mother. Even Della remarked, "Gee! How do we rate all this service? What's come over you, Thelma?"

But Thelma only smiled and glanced over at Wynelle and then grew pink.

Mona came in while they were all talking, heard a smattering of the story, swore unconcernedly and went off to bed.

Cousin Dick did not get in until long after midnight. When he came he was haggard and fiercely irritable. Wynelle, lying awake, could hear his angry rumble and Alberta's interrupting whine, like ill-assorted instruments in an inharmonious orchestra. She was sorry for them all, but her heart was with Roger. She fell asleep with a prayer for him on her lips.

Something woke her just before dawn. She was not aware of having heard any sound, but it seemed as if her name had been spoken. She was alert in an instant and half rose up in bed. Everything was silent but out of habit she ran her hand along the window sill close to the screen where Roger used to slip his notes when she was sick. Sure enough, she could feel the square corner of an envelope.

Moving softly lest she waken Mona, she pushed up the screen until she could pull her letter in. Then she reached under her pillow for her flashlight, snuggling down under the covers so that the light would not disturb Mona.

She felt as if she wanted to hug the very paper the note was written on.

"Dear Wyn:

I have something to tell you that won't wait. If you find this before I have to leave at eight come on out. I'll be waiting.

Yours,

Roger."

Wynelle glanced at her watch. Only five o'clock! They would have a good long time to talk. Stealthily she crept out from the covers and climbed over the foot of the bed leaving Mona deep in snores.

In less than five minutes she was dressed and tiptoeing out the front door, breathless with eagerness. The crisp air braced her senses alertly. She darted a glance around and just made out the outlines of a small car on the far side of the street. Then all at once its lights went on and a tall figure came toward her.

"Hi!" he greeted her joyously, seizing both her arms as if he wanted to swallow her up. He put her in the car and off they went. He gave her hand another glad squeeze just for the joy of having her there.

"Boy! Am I glad you woke up! I was afraid you'd sleep late and we'd have to wait until tonight."

"I'm glad, too!" she answered snuggling down and hugging her knees the way she did when she was content.

He could see the shining of her eyes in the dim light. There was a sweet sense of comradeship upon them both.

"Wait till you hear what happened!" he said exuberantly. And he told her about the visit with Dr. Anderson. She gave little squeals of delight as he went on and when he had finished she cried, "Oh, it seems just too good to be true, doesn't it! I have prayed so that your father would find the Lord!"

"Have you really?" he said in wonder taking her hand in his. "Say! Your hands are cold! Why, you're shivering! Here, this thing sure comes in handy."

He stopped the car and reached to the back shelf for his sweater just as he had that other time. But now he helped her on with it tenderly.

"I g-guess I'm j-just excited," she chattered half laughing and half crying with joy.

"Wait till you hear the rest of the story and you *will* be excited," he told her jubilantly. And he told her about his mother. His hand still lingered on her shoulders and now he drew her close to him. She turned her radiant face up to his.

"How marvelous!" she breathed.

"And not only that," he went on in a voice deep with emotion, "but I'll tell you the best of all." He was holding her hand in his and her heart was pounding.

"Little Wyn," he said, "I have found somebody who would like to share your little brown house with you!"

Wynelle caught her breath in a gasp of disappointment. Business! At a time like this!

"I'll have to know first," he added eagerly, "whether you'll be satisfied with him or not."

He was looking down earnestly into her face in the faint light that was beginning to show in the east.

"*Him!*" she exclaimed.

"Yes," he said humbly with his soul in his eyes.

Then all at once it dawned on her what he meant. "Oh!" she cried and buried her face on his breast. His arms went around her and his lips found hers. A long moment he held her so and then he drew back a little and looked into her eyes.

"Are you *sure,* dearest? It's not an honorable name I'm asking you to take."

"I am sure!" she answered with a glad ring in her voice. "You have made it the noblest name in all the world. Besides, I love it because it's yours, dear!"

With a radiant smile he drew her to him again.

"My darling!" he murmured. She snuggled close into his arms.

"Hasn't the Lord been wonderful to us!" she exclaimed softly. "I'm glad you taught me to rejoice in the dark, though, before the joy came. I'd have been ashamed to take all this if I hadn't trusted Him when it was dark."

"Oh but you're precious," he said holding her closer. "There never was a girl like you in all the world. You've had some pretty tough tests since you came east but you sure have passed them with flying colors! You will never know what it meant to me that day when you prayed for me in the car. I was just about at the end of my rope."

She beamed at him and then they had to go over the whole story again, remembering all their precious little moments. He had to tell her how many times he had wanted to take her in his arms, and she had to tell him how she had thrilled to his look and his touch, and how she had kept his old sweater in the suit-case under her bed so that she could reach down and pat it at night when she felt lonely. They laughed and cried together until all at once they looked at the time and it was quarter after seven.

He chuckled. "My dad will wonder what on earth has become of me," he said as if he didn't care whether all the world wondered. "Let's run down to that old coffee shop and get a bite of breakfast. Then I'll take you home and pick you up at your office—if you need to go!" He gave a shrug. "And tonight you're to have dinner with me."

"Oh, may I come out and cook dinner for you?" she begged.

"Sure!" he exclaimed with pleasure. "That will be great!"

Hand in hand they went into the coffee shop again, smiling at the same discouraged waitress.

They sat in the same little booth and made their plans.

"We don't need to wait a long time, do we, dear?" Roger asked wistfully. "I've been lonely all my life, I think."

Wynelle could scarcely keep from reaching across the table and putting her arms around him at that. She managed to keep her seat but she let him know by her eyes what she was thinking.

"I'll have to see," she said, "whether I'm really needed at the Snellers'. I think I should consider them, don't you? Now that they are in real trouble?"

He nodded with a worshipful look in his eyes.

"I guess so," he agreed. "But don't make it too long." He grinned boyishly.

"I'll see how things are," she said smiling rapturously. "I'll try to keep things going at the office, if there still is an office!"

"It looks to me as if what I always suspected is true," he replied thoughtfully, "that our friend Sneller is tied up with a lot of crooks, and a good many of them are going to get a well-earned vacation in the pen, including him. I can't be glad, for I know what disgrace means more than most people. I couldn't wish it for anybody. But if they put them away it may save a lot of people from being fleeced."

Wynelle nodded. "Several things happened at the office that seemed sort of shady to me, but I wasn't sure enough of law to know."

"There will be plenty uncovered, I guess, in this probe. It's a good thing. But how about Della?"

"I don't know. If the story she told me is true I guess she won't come out too badly, but it won't be fun. She is more scared of having to testify in court than she is ashamed, I believe. She seems to have her standards all awry."

"I suppose she needed a stiff lesson," he said. "I doubt if there will be more than a heavy fine, though. Let me know if I can help."

Wynelle's eyes shone.

"It's that sort of thing I meant when I said you had made Blackstone the noblest name I ever heard," she told him.

He smiled humbly. "That is only grace," he reminded her.

"What's grace?" she asked.

"Undeserved kindness. Didn't God have to show grace to me?" he smiled.

"*And* me," she added.

"Well, anyway," concluded Roger, "we'll do all we can to help and maybe some of them will get to know the Lord."

They hurried home to start the day.

Wynelle found the Snellers wrangling as much as ever, all except Thelma. She found time to give her a little loving squeeze and say, "You've discovered that He keeps His word, haven't you?"

Thelma gave her a bright smile. "It looks like it," she answered shyly.

And when Thelma came home the next day even her looks were changed. Her owlish glasses were gone, and her long-haired Alice-in-Wonderland look. Her hair had been trimmed and it waved gently about her face. She looked more like a little girl than she ever had.

"I am done with that old Thelma," she explained to Wynelle. "I never did like her anyway!" They both laughed, then Thelma confessed: "I got a lot of teasing in school today, just like you said I would. Everybody wanted to know if I wasn't all upset by the tale in the papers this morning and when I tried to tell them why I wasn't they *roared!* They yelled, 'Thelma's got religion! Whaddaya know!' They made a paper cross and hung it around my neck and tried to make me get down on my knees and say my prayers. It wasn't fun." There were tears in her eyes but she managed a brave smile.

Wynelle gave her a warm hug and a kiss. "It may be hard for a while, but don't be afraid," she told her. "The Lord will mean all the more to you when it's over."

When Richard came home from his night work he announced
that he was going to enlist.

"I can't take this mess," he spat out, as if he were too holy for
his family. Wynelle found herself feeling grateful that he was
going.

The wedding was set for a Saturday two weeks ahead.

"We'll ask Dr. Anderson to save the date. Let's make it just a
quiet little wedding," suggested Wynelle, and Roger nodded, well
content. "I'll write mother and Sarah Jane but I'm sure they
won't want to make the trip, with the new baby and all. So I'll ask
Thelma to be my bridesmaid. I've really come to love her, strange
as it may seem!"

Roger swung her around and took her in his arms again.

"Oh, I can't believe that this precious little house is to be our
home," she said, beaming ecstatically about her. They were standing near Grandmother Williams' old secretary. "These things are
all so lovely, just what I would have wanted, if I'd had the
choice."

"Yes, gram prized them," said Roger happily. "This desk is a
hundred and fifty years old, she told me."

"It looks as if it ought to have a secret drawer and treasure!"
laughed Wynelle.

"I think it does have a secret drawer," responded Roger gaily.
"I don't know about the treasure." He pulled out a thin panel
cleverly disguised.

"Why!" exclaimed Wynelle, "here is a letter in it! Maybe it *is*
a fortune!"

They drew it out and opened it. It was addressed not to Roger
but to Wynelle, in her grandmother's fine handwriting. It was
characteristically brief. They stood close together to read it.

"Dear Wynelle: If you ever find this it will be after I am gone
and you may only smile at an old lady's whim.

"When I decided to leave my little brown house to you, I hoped
that you would come east to see it, because I was anxious for you

to meet my boy Roger. Perhaps by the time you read this you or he will be already married. But if you are both free it is my hope that you may learn to love each other.

"Anyway, it has given me pleasure to think of you both sharing the little brown house and making it Home.

My love to you both,

Gram."

When they finished reading Roger had to take Wynelle in his arms again and kiss the happy tears away.

"It's just like her," he said tenderly. "And you are just like her, dearest, only more so!" They laughed.

"I'm glad," she said lovingly, snuggling close to him, "that we can both go on in *our* little brown house together!"